Shattered Eagles
Balkan Fragments

Shattered Eagles
Balkan Fragments

T.J. Winnifrith

Duckworth

For Jo

who refused to be fragmented

First published in 1995 by
Gerald Duckworth & Co. Ltd.
The Old Piano Factory
48 Hoxton Square, London N1 6PB
Tel: 0171 729 5986
Fax: 0171 729 0015

A catalogue record for this book is available
from the British Library.

ISBN 0 7156 2635 3

Typeset by Ray Davies
Printed in Great Britain by
Redwood Books Limited, Trowbridge

Contents

Maps

Preface

This book has been written at odd moments in the last four years. Some chapters have been developed from lectures I gave during these years. Some recount Balkan adventures squeezed in between writing these lectures and carrying out the normal duties of an English university lecturer. We hear much of the onerous nature of these duties; perhaps those who complain about such burdens might care to exchange with their equivalents in the Universities of Sofia, where in 1992 they had one photocopier, or Gjirokastër, where in 1994 they had no typewriters, or Sarajevo, where they had nothing. Nevertheless my inability to give all my attention to Balkan affairs has resulted in the slightly fragmentary nature of this book.

There are other causes of fragmentation. In the summer of 1990 I travelled freely and comfortably through Yugoslavia, though there were vague rumblings of discontent. Gorbachev was firmly entrenched in the Soviet Union, but it was in the same summer in Poland that serious cracks began to appear in the iron curtain. Albania was still a closed book, viewed with regret from the safe haven of Yugoslavia. Albania is now accessible, Yugoslavia unsafe and so fragmented that as with the former Soviet Union I have not risked drawing any new boundaries in my first map.

Just as I was completing this book there appeared two other books which covered some of the same ground. *Bosnia: A Short History* by Noel Malcolm (London, 1994) was deservedly hailed as a masterpiece. Its concentration on Bosnia and its deadly seriousness make this book seem frivolous as well as fragmentary. Malcolm shows how difficult it is in the Balkans to disentangle the present from the past, and yet how important a knowledge of the past is in order to avoid accepting certain myths as fact. He has quite a lot to say about Vlachs, Kosovo and Macedonia, and this shows how difficult it is to write about one part of the Balkans without discussing others. Indeed it is perhaps a danger of the book that by showing quite correctly that Bosnia had an identity of its own and was not a mere geographical expression Malcolm creates two new myths, onto which strident nationalists are likely to latch.

The first myth is that there are really distinct racial groups, Bosnians, Croats, Serbs, Vlachs, Pomaks, Greeks, Albanians, Turks, clearly separated from each other by language, religion and culture for ever and a day. But writing this preface in the mountain villages of Southern Albania, where Vlachs, Greeks and Albanians are inextricably confused, it is obvious that there is no such thing as racial purity. Endogamy of course is the rule rather than the exception in these remote areas, but we all have many ancestors, as Malcolm recognises when he says that there is a large Vlach element in the Serb population.

The second myth that history can bring into play is the idea that one race is superior to another in a particular area if it got there first. There are several obvious examples of this myth in the Balkans. Did the Hungarians or the Romanians occupy Transylvania first? Southern Albania with its Greek flags in the village churches, and its houses burnt in the Second World War is again a place to demonstrate the tragic folly of this myth. There are Greek-speakers in these villages now, there were more in the past, their places being occupied by recently arrived

Vlachs, but it is hard to know who occupied the land in the eighteenth century or the fourteenth century, although the sadly neglected churches might tell us something. Who knows and who cares? The Greek terrorists who attacked an Albanian border post presumably cared even if they did not know.

Simultaneously with Malcolm's book *The Times* published *The Tribes of Europe* (London, 1994). This book had a distinguished editorial board headed by Felipe Fernandez Armesto. It was brightly and clearly set out, with a host of maps, and did have the merit of bringing fragmented minorities to the world's attention. But there was an odd pecking order for the tribes. In Western Europe we had the Cornish and the Manx, the Burgenlanders in Austria, the Prussians in Germany, and perhaps most oddly the Normans, listed with the Scandinavians as if they were really Norsemen. In Eastern Europe the Vlachs and the Pomaks are not listed. They do appear in the index, but then so do the Tats and Teptiyars, Tennyson, Thatcher and Thucydides, the first two obscure minorities, the last three less obscure, but hardly minorities. I feel that such a book trivialises the whole issue of ethnic fragments; the Cornish are not going to murder policemen in Devon.

I end this preface on a suitably sour note, and pass to the more pleasant task of acknowledging help from various quarters. I have received financial assistance in making various visits from the British Academy, the British Council, the European Humanities Research Centre and the Conference and Research Fund of the University of Warwick. The Scouloudi Foundation helped with publication. I must thank Jean Dowling for her admirable maps, Gaynor Kennard and Cheryl Cave for their patient typing. At Duckworth Deborah Blake and Colin Haycraft were towers of strength and support. Among fellow travellers in the Balkans I must single out my wife Helen, my daughter

Naomi, Maurice Byrne, Nicholas Mclintock and Lala Meredith-Vula, who supplied the photograph for the dust jacket. In America I was helped and given hospitality by Nick Balamaci and Socrates Asteriou, in Australia by the family Ciolacou, in Greece by Michael Karamichas, in Romania by the Deac family, in Albania by the Dhamaj and Kotoni family, by Elida Reci and Spiro Shituni. For other kinds of help I must thank John Allcock, Antony Bryer, Richard Clogg, Richard Crompton, Jeff Hilton, Stephen Hill, Stephen Nash, Primrose Peacock, Ann Selby and many others who flattered a battered traveller on his shattered Balkan way.

T.J.W.

1

Fragments

Fragment like *fracture* comes from the Latin word to break, and in the past five years we have seen both the Soviet Union and Yugoslavia breaking and rebreaking. Politics and economics are partial causes of this disintegration, but religion and language, culture and history are the main reasons why so many people in Eastern Europe have struggled and are struggling, often violently and sometimes successfully, to free themselves from the domination of other groups. Fragment does suggest the scrapheap, but the word 'minorities' also has a slightly pejorative connotation and is sometimes numerically inexact. The Albanians in Kosovo and the coloured people of South Africa comprise well over four-fifths of the population, and yet, probably rightly, those who support the Albanians and the ANC do so in the name of minority rights.

When I say I am interested in minorities, people often assume that I am talking about women or homosexuals or other groups disadvantaged by society, whose troubles, deplorable though they be, have nothing to do with the wars of Eastern Europe. It might seem easy to preface minorities with an adjective to distinguish the Slovenes and Macedonians from women and homosexuals, but the choice of the adjective is a hard one.

Ethnic, once a term for fashionable if mildly eccentric clothing, has become hideously abused as a result of the Orwellian euphemism, *ethnic cleansing*. In the best of worlds *ethnic* was a vague term, suggesting some old-fashioned and distasteful concepts of blood and race. These concepts are inaccurate in the Balkans. It is true that one finds villages whose inhabitants show distinct reluctance to have their daughters marry outside the village, let alone someone speaking a different language or belonging to a different faith. But, especially in the towns, mixed marriages are not all that uncommon, nor can they have been in the past. Dark-skinned Greek Orthodox-speakers of Greek, fair-haired Islamic-speakers of Turkish, Slav-speakers who are either totally black or have straight noses as in a Minoan fresco, all give the lie to any idea of an ethnic stereotype or any notion of racial purity. There is the added complication, very relevant to Greece's troubles, that *ethnos* in Greek means a nation, and thus the Greeks are frightened to admit having ethnic minorities, fearing national minorities like Trojan horses within their midst.

Linguistic and religious groupings are easier to determine, although not that easy, and curiously confused with each other. In the former Yugoslavia Catholic Slovenia and to a lesser extent Orthodox Macedonia formed reasonably distinct entities, religiously and linguistically, and did not find it all that difficult to break away. But the Croats, the Serbs and the Bosnians all speak the same language, and the present war in Bosnia and past and future wars between Croats and Serbs would seem to be caused by religion. It is true that the Croats and Serbs use a different alphabet and have a different history, but language is not wholly at the root of present troubles. Serbia still rules a large Hungarian and Romanian population; it is the Albanian population of Kosovo with their Islamic population who present more difficulties.

In the Caucasus there is tension between the Christian Armenians and Islamic Azeris, but language as well as religion is involved in a region where there is a mosaic of

EUROPEAN FRAGMENTS

A capital letter indicates a
fragment of considerable importance.
a small letter a minor fragment

A	Albanian	gg	Gagauz	s	Swedish
al	Alsatian	Gr	Greek	Sa	Sardinian
B	Basque	H	Hungarian	sl	Slovene
br	Breton	I	Lapp	sg	Scots Gaelic
C	Catalan	la	Ladin	sm	Slav Macedonian
co	Corsican	o	Occitan	T	Turkish
d	Danish	P	Pomak	ts	Tsakonian
e	Erse or Irish Gaelic	po	Polish	V	Vlach
f	French	R	Romanian	W	Welsh
fr	Frisian	ro	Romansch	we	Wendish / Sorb
g	German	ru	Ruthenian		

| 0 | 500 | 1000km |

Map 1

linguistic groups in an area with not enough sovereign states to accommodate them all even if it were the case, as it is not, that the members of these sovereign states lived in areas adjacent to each other. Elsewhere in the former Soviet Union states have broken away from Russia mainly on linguistic grounds. There are distinct languages known as Estonian, Latvian and Lithuanian, and fairly distinct languages known as White Russian and Ukrainian. Religion, not exactly encouraged since the end of the First World War in Slav Russia and since the end of the Second World War in the former Baltic republics, is not a very potent force. But there are complications with language. Slav languages do not differ very much from each other. In the Soviet Union, as in Yugoslavia, neighbouring villages understand each other, although at the end of the spectrum Ruthenian-speakers do not understand Russian, nor do Slovene-speakers comprehend people from Macedonia.[1] And then both socialist states encouraged and in some cases forced people to move into the remote parts of these states. Hence we have small numbers of Serbs in Slovenia and Macedonia, and, more worryingly and more distantly, a large number of Russian speakers in the Baltic states and the Crimea.

Language and religion are oddly mixed in other parts of the Balkans. A chapter of this book is devoted to the Pomaks, Islamic Bulgarian-speakers. A hundred years ago the main war in Macedonia was between Patriarchists, supporters of the Greek church, and Exarchists, supporters of the Bulgarian church. Some Exarchists spoke Greek, more Patriarchists spoke Bulgarian. The struggle was originally over what language should be used in church, and in the schools which the churches organised. Later it was a struggle over boundaries. Population exchanges in the first quarter of this century ensured that on the whole Greek churches and Greek schools predominated south of the Greek-Bulgarian border, established in 1913, and Bulgarian churches and schools north of the border, but there were still, and still are, speakers of a kind of Bulgarian many miles south of the frontier. In Albania the reverse is the case. Most Albanian-speakers in Greece have either left or been forced to leave, but there is still a substantial Greek-speaking minority in Albania. This minority is of course Orthodox, but there is also a large Albanian-speaking Orthodox population. There are also Vlach- and Slav-speakers among the Orthodox population. Ethnological statistics are clearly very difficult to obtain in such a situation, made more difficult by bilingualism, a remote mountainous terrain, the banning of all religion by Enver Hoxha, the frequent migrations since the collapse of the Hoxha regime and the general political unreliability of the Balkans.

Clearly neither *linguistic* nor *religious* nor *ethnic* is a suitable adjective to clarify the unsuitable term 'minority'. The more tragic *'fragment'* sounds poetic, but to illustrate it in its Balkan context it might perhaps be useful to consider such fragments in the rest of Europe. Most of these fragments are linguistic rather than religious, although the best known, certainly for English readers, is what could be called the Catholic fragment in Northern Ireland or the Protestant fragment in Ireland, depending upon what side is taken in this particular controversy. Language hardly enters the picture; attempts by members of the IRA to learn Gaelic and give themselves Gaelic names have a comic rather than a tragic air in a far from comic conflict. Elsewhere in Western Europe there is a small religious element in the struggle between Flemish and Walloon in Belgium, and various rather tame-seeming religious squabbles in multilingual Switzerland.[2] It might seem like a token of hope for a multi-cultural Europe that in Strasbourg, scene of conflicts between Protestant and

Catholic, Germans and French, it is possible to attend services in both German and French in neighbouring Protestant and Catholic cathedrals.

Elsewhere in the European community it has been calculated that a sixth of the population speaks a language other than one of the official nine. This figure, like all figures, is suspect in its elasticity, a particular elastic quality being provided by the willingness to equate dialect with language. There is also an important difference between languages which are spoken in one country, and are the historic language of another country, and languages which have no external support.

Curiously the external support is not always a help, since the major-state language can drive out the minority dialect, as seems to be happening with French in the Channel Islands, German in Alsace and even on a very small scale Greek in southern Italy. None of these particular fragments seem to be causing much conflict or indeed much interest, and in terms of human suffering these groups cannot really compare with immigrant workers from the Caribbean, Asia and Africa who come to live in Europe, indigenous or immigrant populations in the Americas, where English, Spanish and Portuguese drive down native languages, native languages in Africa faced with arbitrary linguae francae owing to the whim of Imperial boundary makers, vast areas of Asia where nation states like China and India encompass a whole variety of tongues, and people persecuted for their religion all over the world. In this world of woe European fragments have perhaps not received their due, and it might be as well to list them.

In the British Isles Welsh, Scots Gaelic and Irish Gaelic are spoken by a relatively small proportion even of Wales, Scotland and Ireland, and of course a very small proportion of the total number of people in the British Isles. Exact

numbers are hard to calculate. Irish Gaelic is encouraged
by the Government, and many (perhaps a million) learn
and speak a few words, but as few as twenty thousand
speak the language habitually, and the same number
probably is true of Scots Gaelic. Welsh has about a quarter
of a million speakers, but sadly in all these cases habitual
speakers of the language seem to be decreasing, monoglot
speakers have almost vanished, and the future of the
languages looks bleak in spite of careful and imaginative
efforts to foster them, a great contrast to the efforts to
suppress them in the eighteenth and nineteenth centuries.
In the last decade Manx has died, joining Cornish which
died in the eighteenth century, and Norn, a Scandinavian
dialect of the Shetlands which lasted a little longer. The
French patois of the Channel Islands cannot survive much
longer.[3]

In France there is a variety of minority languages,
treated rather less sympathetically than in Britain.
Breton suffered as a result of the Second World War, as
did Alsatian, now paradoxically under threat because of
the easy access to Alsace of proper German-speakers.
Corsican has a rather dubious status. Provençal or Occitan
with its glorious heritage from the Middle Ages suffers
badly through having no centre: it is spoken in scattered
pockets over a wide area. Oddly it is the official language
of a small part of Catalonian Spain. Suppression under
Franco appeared to strengthen Basque in Spain, much
stronger than in France, as well as Catalan and Gallego,
another language with a rich literary tradition. Indeed
Spain, in spite or because of political pressure, appears to
be leaning over backwards to accommodate its minority
languages, even being prepared to admit Andalucian in
the south and Cantabrian in the north to some kind of
rights, although these surely are dialects. The difficult
distinction between dialect and language is important in

Italy where the spoken language around Florence has become the literary language, very different from what is spoken in Sicily, Sardinia or Friuli, probably different languages, and fairly different from what is spoken in Naples or Piedmont, probably different dialects. In addition Italy contains a small number of French, Provençal, German, Ladin, Slav, Greek, Catalan (in Sardinia) and Albanian speakers. There used to be trouble with German speakers in the southern Tyrol near the Brenner Pass, but this seems to have died down. In general Italy is tolerant towards its minorities, in contrast to Greece which refuses to recognise that it has Albanian-, Vlach- or Slav-speakers, and only admits to Turkish-speakers as a religious minority. On the other hand Greece is very keen to stress the presence of Greek-speakers in other countries.[4]

Belgium's bilingualism threatens to tear the nation apart; there is also a small German fragment in Belgium. Holland and Germany have a small Frisian minority which keeps its identity. The German-Danish border is not quite synonymous with the linguistic border, but the only real fragment in Germany apart from numerous gastarbeiter are the Sorbs or Wends east of Dresden. There used to be many German speakers in Eastern Europe, but most of these returned, or were forced to return, in or after the Second World War. Switzerland with its four official languages and preservation of Romansch looks like a model for a plurilingual society, but Romansch is declining, and Switzerland is not without linguistic and religious tensions. In Scandinavia there is an odd problem with Norway's two languages, a Swedish minority in Finland and a considerable Lapp population. Denmark has a Faroese fragment and Eskimo-speakers in Greenland. Austria incorporates small Hungarian and Croat groups, and a thin sausage-skin of Slovene-speakers at the southern end of sausage-shaped Carinthia, where there was a plebiscite after the First World War.[5]

Thus in every Western country apart from Portugal, where everybody speaks Portuguese, and Luxemburg, where almost everybody speaks a kind of French and a kind of German, there are indigenous fragments. Most countries in Western Europe do not regard these fragments as very important, especially in these post-Maastricht days when they are striving for greater union. The groups that do cause them concern are the ethnic immigrants from former imperial territories, the gastarbeiter in Germany, and now a flood of refugees from Eastern Europe. Nevertheless Western Europeans can recognise fragments in their midst, even if they try to marginalise them into the realm of folklore.

With Eastern Europe it is rather different. Here the Russian, Austro-Hungarian and Turkish empires were multi-ethnic states, very difficult to divide. Treaty-makers after the First World War did their best, although there was a slight tendency to reward the victor. Hungary and Bulgaria did badly, Romania and Greece well. Even the most ingenious treaty-maker could deal not with fragments far away from the major bloc of population or fragments too small or disorganised to form a nation state. Thus the Germans of Eastern Europe, Hungarians of Transylvania, Albanians of Greece, Vlachs, Pomaks and Gypsies were left to fend for themselves. Hitler and Stalin by brutality rather than ingenuity succeeded in removing some of these fragments through persecution and transportation. Briefly during the Second World War Hungary regained Transylvania and the Italian regime in Albania ruled Kosovo. When the frontiers were redrawn after the Second World War, some of the anomalies had vanished, but others had been put in their place. The Soviet Union had after 1945 swallowed a great many non-Slav areas.

Under Communism the ethnic problems of Eastern Europe remained frozen. There were of course rivalries between countries and rivalries between different groups in countries, but, as the official line was the common good and the brotherhood of man, such rivalries could not be encouraged. Tito almost succeeded in uniting Yugoslavia. The Soviet Union did allow different groups to have their own socialist republics. Nevertheless tensions did remain; old scores were waiting to be settled. In contrast to Western Europe, there was no fresh intake of immigrants or gastarbeiter to act as a distracting force.

The various Communist regimes did do quite a lot to break up petty rivalries for the good of the state. They moved people from villages to the towns – architectural disasters, but easier places in which to fuse disparate groups. They discouraged religion, sadly a source of discord. Their motives may not always have been pure, and perhaps the period of suppression may have served to exacerbate pent-up feelings.

At all events Eastern Europe is a minefield of potential disasters quite apart from the actual disasters in the Caucasus and Yugoslavia. There are Russian-speakers, once a majority, now a minority in the newly independent states. Lithuania also has a Polish fragment. The frontiers and ethnic composition of Moldova make no sense. The Dobrudja and northern Bulgaria have always been a mosaic of different races including some eccentric fragments like the Lipovanes with their strange religious beliefs, Tartars, non-Ottoman Turks, and the Gagauz, non-Islamic Turks. There are still some Germans in Romania and Hungary. The Banat in Romania and Yugoslavia is still a kaleidoscope of different groups, living it has to be said in some degree of amity, unlike the Hungarians in Romania. Some Jews and Gypsies succeeded in surviving

Nazi persecution; regrettably there is still anti-Semitism, and the Gypsies are not popular.

In my wanderings in the Balkans I have come across odd little pockets scarcely known even to philologists, such as the Ciri Biri or Istrian Vlachs of north-western Yugoslavia or the cave dwellers of Didymoteichon in north-eastern Greece. I have come across a great deal of bilingualism and multilingualism, whole villages which are trilingual, and one man who claimed to speak eight languages and could write none of them. It is very hard to delineate linguistic groups. It is easier to speak more than one language than to have more than one religion, and that is perhaps why religion rather than language may seem more important. On the other hand it is easier to conceal one's religion than one's language and that is why linguistic fragments also remain a cause for concern and of conflict.

Most of the languages I have mentioned are fairly moribund. Irish Gaelic in spite of strong state support has rapidly retreated to the very remotest parts of the west coast, although a century ago it was commonly spoken in most of the western half of the island. Vlach receives no encouragement from any Balkan government, and yet stubbornly holds out in the same villages where its presence was noted a century ago. But these villages have sadly diminished numbers, and again and again I noted in Greece that the old spoke the language, people of my generation understood it, and the young thought it silly. In Albania the position was slightly better, with middle-aged people being forced to work so hard that the children learnt the languages from their grandparents. Vlach does not have much going for it. It has no standardised alphabet, little literature and no state support. But it has one great advantage; it is competing against a multiplicity of tongues, Greek, Albanian, Macedonian, some of which have only recently gained recognition as languages. Irish on the other hand has only one competitor, the all-embracing English. When I wrote *The Vlachs* (London: Duckworth, 1987) I concluded that there were about fifty thousand speaking Vlach in the Balkans. This was before I had visited Albania properly; I now think there are about a hundred thousand. Vlachs would increase the number.[6] Nevertheless the future of Vlach is as bleak as that of Irish.

The death of a language is a subject for sorrow. We regret the vanishing of rare species of birds and whales, and should regret the passing of rare languages. A variety of languages adds to the richness of life. If Irish and Vlach go the way of Cornish and Manx, will it not soon be the turn of Danish and Dutch? How dull and how dreadful it would be if the whole world spoke nothing but bad English.

There are of course arguments on the other side. A universal language like Esperanto has been seen as an instrument for world peace. The Tower of Babel gets a bad press. Those who seek to thrust minority languages down people's throats are often guilty of the same kind of persecution as was perpetrated against them in the past. Welsh and Catalan are two comparatively healthy languages in spite of, or perhaps because of, a period when they were frowned upon. There are places in Wales where English-speakers are forced to learn Welsh at school, and the same is true of Castilian speakers in Catalonia. Is this right?

There are other problems too. Languages rich in medieval literature like Gallego and Scots Gaelic do not adapt well to the needs of the twentieth century. This makes them unpopular with the young, upon whom their fate depends. Many lesser-used languages are spoken by the simple and uneducated, but promoted by intellectuals who are often fluent in other languages. There is in Macedonia a school of Vlach poets; they also write in Macedonian. Scots Gaelic poets turn their hand to English poetry. Indeed there is some evidence to show that bilingualism increases literacy and linguistic skill.[7] This is some argument for encouraging English school children to learn Welsh. The Irish like to think that a long line of wordsmiths and wits from Swift to Seamus Heaney are unconscious inheritors of a Gaelic as well as an Anglo-Irish past. On the other hand bilingual countries like Switzerland, Belgium and Canada are not notorious for their literary achievements.

But it could be argued that it is the right of everyone to speak and read and have access to the literary heritage of the language they spoke as children, and to choose whatever faith they wish. People in trouble need help, and the first kind of help they need is that the truth about their plight should be known. There is a great deal of misinformation about linguistic minorities. In his excellent book *The Death of the Irish Language* (London: Routledge, 1990) R. Hindley draws attention to the weakness of other studies, although his own figures for minorities other than Irish Gaelic are probably too gloomy. He does show the tendency of linguistic fragments to exaggerate their own numbers and the gap, perhaps most notable among the Irish, between habitual speakers of a language and people who appear in statistics as having some acquaintance with the language. *The Encyclopaedia of Minorities* (London: Longman, 1992) not only strays into non-linguistic or religious minorities (i.e. low-caste inhabitants of Japan and India), but also aiming for its world coverage is inaccurate in particular parts of the globe, notably Eastern Europe. A Catalan map of linguistic groups in Europe mentions Cornish and Manx as extinct languages being re-established, but has no word of Vlach.[8] It carefully marks the Occitan-speaking valley in Catalonia (the two languages are very similar and both French and Spanish are also spoken there), but crudely divides the former Yugoslavia between the Croats and the Serbs, although the two languages are virtually the same apart from the alphabet; there are many other languages spoken in Yugoslavia, and the actual division between the Serbs and the Croats in no way corresponds to the line in the map. A project sponsored by the European community on minorities produced papers full of information on Italian and Spanish minorities, but distinctly weak on others: the authors were Italian. Even more specialised studies like that of H. Poulton, *The Balkans: Minorities and States in Conflict* (London: Minority Rights Publishers, 1991) are not without error, all too easy as I know in an area both inaccessible and volatile.

A case could be made out, as these partial inaccurate studies show, for more cooperation between linguistic groups. Religious groups understandably find cooperation difficult. Celtic groups do meet, and the Galicians as honorary if slightly bogus Celts are invited. I have attended a conference on bilingualism in Western Europe; it was broken up by extreme Catalan nationalists. I have been invited to a conference for Central European minorities. An interesting link has been established between the University of Tromsö in Norway studying Lapps and the University of Sofia studying Bulgarian minorities. The Bureau for Lesser Used Languages based in Dublin with a small budget does its best for a variety of linguistic groups. Language fragments of a major language sometimes receive help from the state where that language is spoken, but this can be dangerous politically. Even when it is not, there can still be dangers for the language fragment concerned, as it is likely to be assimilated to the major language.

Political action by and on behalf of these fragments is difficult. Many of the groups I have named have lost sympathy and support through political action that it is unwise, sometimes violent and sometimes impracticable.

A minority that has become a majority, a fraction that is turned upside down, is often guilty of the same crimes as were practised against it.

This book offers no easy political solutions. In that sense it is as incomplete as the few fragments it attempts to describe. The Vlachs are one of the more successful fragments in the Balkans, both in preserving their language against all the odds and in avoiding too many political conflicts. Perhaps they offer some kind of solution. Other fragments or fragmented areas are described because so little is known about them, or because so much of what is known is based on partial and biased sources. To comprehend all in the Balkans is not to pardon all, since there is too much to forgive, but a little comprehension might bring about a great deal more compassion.[9]

2

Balkan Latinity

In Western Europe we have a long tradition of interest in the Latin language and Roman history. France, Italy, Spain and Portugal speak languages derived from Latin, and in Germany, Holland and Britain Latin still plays an important role in the school curriculum, although the influence of Latin is waning as it is in the Roman Catholic Church. In Britain we still get excited about minor archaeological discoveries of Roman remains, forgetting in our enthusiasm that Britain was a very unimportant Province of the Roman Empire, the last in Western Europe to be conquered in 43 AD and the first in 410 AD to be abandoned.

It is all very different in Eastern Europe. Here history and economics have dictated that little interest is paid to the Latin language or to Roman history. The mighty Roman fortress of Naissus preserves its name in modern Niš, but the site is virtually unexcavated; more interest is paid to a rather grisly monument in Niš of skulls of Serbs murdered by the Turks. Sir Arthur Evans, the excavator of Knossos, did important work tracing Roman remains in Bosnia over a century ago, and ran into certain political difficulties in so doing.[1] Little work has been done since, and the political difficulties remain. In Greece important Roman sites lie comparatively neglected in the face of competition from Ancient Greek sites around them or beneath them. In Ancient and Medieval times the East was richer than the West, but this is obviously not the case

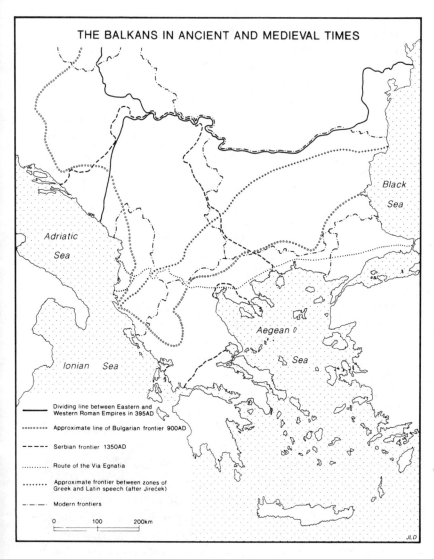

THE BALKANS IN ANCIENT AND MEDIEVAL TIMES

Black Sea

Adriatic Sea

Ionian Sea

Aegean Sea

Dividing line between Eastern and Western Roman Empires in 395AD

Approximate line of Bulgarian frontier 900AD

Serbian frontier 1350AD

Route of the Via Egnatia

Approximate frontier between zones of Greek and Latin speech (after Jireček)

Modern frontiers

0   100   200km

Map 2

now, and it is understandable that the governments of East European countries should have little money as well as little time for exploring distant links with a culture with which they have little in common.

But of course a language derived from Latin does survive in modern Romania and in scattered mountainous pockets in the centre of the Balkan peninsula. At first sight this seems paradoxical. Romania was under Roman rule for less than two hundred years, and the places in which the Aroumanians or Vlachs of the central Balkans are to be found are either so remote that one might think that Latin would have had difficulty in penetrating there or so far south that Latin might have quickly succumbed to the stronger influence of Greek.

My answer to this paradox is to propose that the influence of Latin in the Balkans was much larger than has been commonly supposed. The extent of this influence has been diminished by the lack of interest in things Roman in Eastern Europe, and its replacement by a rather deplorable nationalist bias. We can detect this bias by examining the theories of certain historians as to the origins of the pockets of the Latin language to be found in odd spots in the central Balkans, the people known rather vaguely as Vlachs and Aroumanians, or by a host of local names.[2]

For the Greeks these people are indisputably Greek, the descendants they like to think of Roman soldiers, set to guard the high passes, who married local girls and begat Latin-speaking children. Such a theory ignores the absence of any evidence of a Roman military presence in most of these areas, and the worrying fact that one learns languages at one's mother's knee rather than one's father's. For the Romanians the Vlachs are Romanians, who at some stage between the sixth and tenth centuries split off from the main body of the Romanians mysteriously preserving their identity north of the Danube, although such a theory ignores the inherent improbability that anyone would wish to abandon the plains of the Danube for inaccessible mountainous villages further south. For the Hungarians, anxious to prove that they got to Transylvania first, the Vlachs live in the original dwelling place of the Romanians, who only came to live north of the Danube in the late Middle Ages when they first begin to appear in history, although there is no evidence of this unlikely northern migration. And for some of the Vlachs themselves, now beginning to take an interest in their own history, they represent the original stock of the central Balkans: I have met Vlachs eager to claim Alexander the Great and even Aeneas as their ancestor.

The history of the Balkans in the early Middle Ages is difficult to write because we have so little written evidence of what happened except around Constantinople. It is clear that there were many movements of population. We have some evidence of when cities were abandoned in the Dark Ages following the Slav invasions, and even of what language was written in these cities, although of course the written language, Greek or Latin, may not have been the same as that spoken. Anxiety to prove autochthony is a little absurd in view of this uncertainty about evidence, the degree of migration and the likelihood of mixed marriages.

The Roman conquest of the Balkan peninsula is fairly well chronicled thanks to the historian Livy. It proceeded surprisingly quickly, to the extent that, within two hundred years of the initial involvement almost by accident of Rome with the piratical queen Teuta on the Adriatic coast near Kotor, Rome had control of most of the Balkans south of the Danube. In Augustus' reign the future Emperor Tiberius fought some hard campaigns in northern Yugoslavia and in the east of the Balkans Thrace was still a client kingdom until the reign of Claudius. Dacia, across the Danube, had to wait for Roman rule until the reign of the Emperor Trajan at the end of the first century, and archaeological evidence suggests that he did not conquer the whole of Romania.

A strong military presence was necessary in the southern Balkans in the centuries before Christ and along the Danube frontier in the centuries thereafter. Three battles in the civil wars at the end of the Republic were fought in the southern Balkans at Pharsalus, Philippi and Actium. Roman cities like Nicopolis in Greek Epirus were founded, Roman military settlements were made at places like Dium in Greek Thessaly. The building of the Via Egnatia across the Balkans ensured that Roman citizens could travel easily, and we hear of famous Romans in the Balkans. Virgil died en route for Greece, Horace lost his shield at Philippi, Ovid spent the last years of his life in exile on the Danube, Cicero's friend Atticus had vast estates in Epirus to which the orator temporarily retired when he was exiled, and the death of Caesar found his great-nephew Augustus quietly studying at Apollonia in modern Albania.

These early links have encouraged some to find fanciful traces of a permanent Latin-speaking population in the Balkans. Thus the Farsheroti, a name for quite a large section of the Aroumanian population, are supposed to gain their name from the legionaries of Pompey defeated at Pharsalus, where Vlachs are also to be found, although the Farsherots would seem to owe their title to the Albanian town of Frashër. The *armata praesidia* of Livy sent to guard the Macedonian borders are supposed to be ancestors of the *armatoles* guarding the mountain passes in the later Ottoman Empire, although the history of the intervening nineteen hundred years hardly suggests an unbroken line of descent. The important literary and historical figures I have mentioned were Romans who learnt

Greek, and even aimed to bring Greek culture to Rome, not Romans who taught the Greeks Latin. Greek would appear to have had something of the cultural superiority over Latin that French had over English in the first half of this century. For the ordinary soldier or trader settled in the Balkans this superiority did not probably matter much, but the evidence of archaeology does suggest that Latin did not last very long in places where Greek was regularly spoken. Similarly in Western Europe former colonies in Spain, and France, Sicily and southern Italy slowly lost their Greek, although tiny fragments of Greek still survive in Apulia and Calabria to this day. But there were great sections of the Balkans where Greek was never a serious contender, and where, as in Western Europe, Latin should have become accepted as the lingua franca. The demarcation line between Greek and Latin, the so-called Jireček line, named after the famous Balkan historian, is based on epigraphic evidence. This runs north of the Via Egnatia across southern Albania where there was a certain amount of bilingualism, southern Macedonia between Scupi (Latin) and Stobi (Greek), and then turns sharply north to leave only northern Bulgaria and the Danube frontier in the Latin sphere of influence. It is in this area that we must look for the cradle of Balkan Latinity. Why should this cradle not have produced future Latin-speakers in the same way as France, Italy, Spain and Portugal? Indeed why did it not produce more Latin speakers, since the Roman Empire lasted longer in these parts, and there was a greater military presence on the Danube than on the Rhine. Roads, cities and trade were the ways in which the Latin language was spread, but though the area is inadequately excavated there seems little evidence that there was less urbanisation in Eastern Europe than in Western Europe. The climate and terrain are rugged in the Balkans, but so they are in parts of Spain, Italy and France.

The division of the Roman Empire into two halves was of course an important event for the future of Latin in the east, coinciding as it almost did with the adoption of Christianity as the official religion of both parts of the Empire. It would be easy to see in this division the death-blow to Latin in the Balkans, since henceforth in the east government, civil, military, educational and ecclesiastical, would be in the hands of the Greeks. But the deathblow was a long time in coming. The Empire was divided, subdivided and occasionally reunited in different ways during the course of the fourth century. Provinces in the western parts of the Balkans, corresponding to Albania and what used to be Yugoslavia, sometimes found themselves in the eastern part of the Roman Empire, sometimes in the west. It is perhaps not entirely surprising that Yugoslavia now should be so fatally divided, or that in Albania, so near to Greece and Italy but able to play off the claims of Greek and Latin, they still speak a language derived from neither.

In the sixth century the Danube frontier still held and, although Greek-speaking Constantinople controlled the administration, Latin-speakers still thrived on this frontier and in the lands behind it north of the Jireček line.[3] Admittedly, the Latin spoken would have been hardly the Latin of Cicero and Virgil, who themselves spoke a language very different from the literary language they wrote. The process of simplification, or as some might call it debasement, of vulgar Latin had been increased by the presence of a large number of people who originally did not speak Latin, barbarian invaders, who as neighbours or mercenaries or captives or unwelcome guests, had found themselves adjacent to or within the borders of the Roman Empire and there picked up a rough kind of Latin. It is possible that the peculiar feature of Balkan Latin, the postpositive article, is an inheritance from the language of these invaders.[4] Ethnologically the composition of this Latin-speaking area must have been a strange hotchpotch with the military element taken from all over the Empire and the civilian element an odd mixture of Thracian, Illyrian and even Celtic tribes mixed up with this military element and the new invaders.

The Danube frontier did not finally break until the disastrous revolt against the Emperor Maurice in the year 602. In the sixth century it had frequently buckled through growing pressure from the Slavs, and there had been earlier invasions by Goths. The frontier had of course been altered in the year 271 when the Emperor Aurelian had decided to withdraw from Dacia north of the Danube, and here belatedly we raise the vexed question of how far a Latin-speaking population took root and continued to live north of the Danube in the years after Aurelian. It is difficult to answer this question very satisfactorily. It seems unlikely that Latin should take all that strong a hold in about a hundred and seventy years and be able to survive for the next seven hundred when it was less successful in the areas further south. On the other hand archaeology and probability would suggest that Aurelian's alteration of the frontier did not lead to a complete evacuation, and there are stray indications of some kind of Latin presence north of the border, although our largely Greek sources do not help by their old-fashioned use of the term *Romaioi* to describe the forces of the Empire, whether they were Greek-speaking or Latin. This term is however a useful reminder that in the sixth century the Roman Empire was still bilingual. Justin and his nephew Justinian were Latin-speakers originating from near Skopje in northern Macedonia. Justinian conquered Italy, southern Spain and northern Africa and thus briefly virtually reunited the empire. Almost certainly he totally overestimated the strength of the Empire, and the Slav invasions which followed removed almost all of the Latin-speaking parts of the Empire in the Balkans from Imperial control. With this fall knowledge of the Latin language disappeared in Constantinople. There is some evidence that even in Greek-speaking parts of the Empire Latin was spoken by some. Johannes Lydus, an odd character, claims it was spoken by magistrates, and Greek historians have seized on this statement as evidence that their bilingual Vlachs have a long and respectable ancestry, although when we meet the Vlachs in medieval records they do seem on the other side of the law. Johannes's magistrates and the chairs of Latin in Constantinople might point to some educated people having Latin as a second language, but hardly to Latin being spoken by the bulk of the population in Greek-speaking areas.

It was different north of the Jireček line and perhaps different north of the Danube. But it was this area and a great deal of the Greek-speaking area that fell a victim to the Slav invasions. We do not know a great deal about these invasions. Our Greek literary sources record them in a melancholy fashion, and archaeology records the sad collapse of cities. The Slavs, apart from a loose tribal organisation, appear to have lacked the political structures of the Western kingdoms, and no doubt this did not help the spread of Latin as a language of administration. Nor thanks to Cyril and Methodius could the Catholic Church have any influence except in the north-west corner of the Balkan peninsula.

But the Latin-speakers whom I have been postulating as living in the northern Balkans must have gone somewhere. To use a rather unfortunate topical analogy, the collapse of Latin in the Balkans can be likened to the collapse of Russian in former Communist countries, where it was once taught as a second language but has now been abandoned in favour of English. The fate of Latin-speakers in the northern Balkans was more like the fate of the Bosnians, scattered as refugees, but still of course speaking their language. We may perhaps hear of some of these refugees in the story of the people of Sirmium recorded in the *Acta Sancti Demetrii*, but otherwise there is little evidence of their existence.

But of course there is little evidence of anything. Latin-speakers are not mentioned by historians between the year 597, just before the collapse of the Danube frontier in the mysterious 'torna, torna' episode situated in south-east Bulgaria, and the year 971 when the brother of the future Bulgarian emperor Samuel was killed by some Vlachs between Kastoria and Prespa. Neither of these incidents need necessarily refer to Latin-speakers, although 'torna, torna, fratre', a confused order, confusingly recorded by two different historians, does have a Latin air about it, and at least some of the references to Vlachs should refer to Latin-speakers. It is not until Kekaumenos writing in the eleventh century that we get a definite connection between Latin-speakers north and south of the Danube.

This sad lack of evidence can however easily be explained. Greek sources are uninterested in languages other than Greek. In addition, for three and a half centuries after the collapse of the Danube frontier the imperial frontier remained well to the south of the Jireček line and, with the Slavs penetrating as far as the Peloponnese, Byzantine sources would have little reason to meet Latin-speakers even if they had been interested in them or known about them. By the time the antiquarian pedant Constantine Porphyrogenitus came to the throne knowledge of Latin had entirely vanished, as is clear from the emperor's inadequate philology. The boundaries of the Empire by Constantine's time had advanced to the Jireček line and in places beyond it, and there are strange mentions by him of odd people in Yugoslavia who may be

Latin-speakers. He is sadly silent on the Bulgarian side of the Balkans.[5]

Basil the Bulgar-slayer's campaigns around the year 1000 finally brought back the Danube frontier which remained the frontier of the Byzantine Empire until the end of the twelth century. It is in these two centuries that mention of the Vlachs becomes frequent in Byzantine sources; sometimes we hear of Vlachs fighting with the Byzantines, more often against them. There is little to prove that all these Vlachs were Latin-speakers, although we do find the odd Latin-sounding proper name, but of course nothing to prove that they weren't. Bulgarian national pride has been reluctant to concede that the second Bulgarian Empire of the Asenids was certainly called a Vlach empire by Byzantine sources. Serbian chauvinism has tended to play down the many mentions of Vlachs in early Serbian records, and Greek historians have tended to play down the large presence of Vlachs in Medieval Thessaly. Given that we find Latin-speaking Vlachs in these areas it seems reasonable to assume a large Latin-speaking presence, recorded in the Middle Ages. Some Vlachs would like to see themselves recorded as Armenians, an unlikely corruption of Aroumanians, but I think that too owes more to chauvinism than to scholarship. There are Armenians settled in the Balkan peninsula in Byzantine times, and this is a useful reminder of how fluid the population was in the multi-ethnic Byzantine Empire, as indeed it was in its Ottoman successor.

In Western Europe we have languages derived from Latin and have evidence, archaeological, literary and linguistic, to trace the development of this language and the civilisations it engendered, albeit the centuries in which these developments took place are known as the Dark Ages. In Eastern Europe darkness took a different form, and for various reasons we do not have the necessary evidence. We therefore have to rely on arguments from analogy, or probability, and from the poor scraps of literary and archaeological evidence that biased medieval and modern authors and authorities have given to us. These arguments and fragments of evidence do suggest that there was a large Latin-speaking population in the northern and central Balkans throughout the period 200 BC – 1200 AD, just as there was certainly a large Latin-speaking presence in the next seven hundred years.

The fourth Crusade in 1204 almost coincided with the rise of the Second Bulgarian or Vlach Empire which reached its height in the first half of the thirteenth century. It is in the next two hundred and fifty years that we hear a good deal about Vlachs, a period when there was no central authority in the Balkans, similar to the nineteenth century when again Vlachs emerge from obscurity into the comparative limelight of historical footnotes. Clearly the Vlachs were involved in the Second Bulgarian Empire. They are mentioned frequently in Serbian records. Byzantine sources draw attention to the Vlachs, sometimes connecting them with Albanian invaders. Thessaly became known as Vlachia. There were virtually independent Vlach states briefly flourishing in the death throes of the Byzantine Empire. Ottoman accounts do distinguish Vlachs from Greeks. Romanian-speakers north of the Danube come out of the shadows, and are connected and confused with Vlachs to the south. Not all accounts of Vlachs necessarily refer to speakers of a Latin language, but the multiplicity of references does suggest a large Latin-speaking presence between 1204 and 1453, and by implication a considerable presence before and after this period.

There are fewer mentions of the Vlachs between the successful siege of Constaninople in 1453 and the last unsuccessful siege of Vienna in 1683, which may be taken as the beginning of the protracted decline and fall of the

Ottoman Empire. The Turks were not much concerned with the subject peoples, and there was little interest in the West. Knowledge of the interior of the Balkans remained rudimentary until the middle of the nineteenth century with, for instance, lakes Ohrid and Prespa being marked badly out of place in most Western maps, and the first Western travellers to these parts still having to struggle with the writings of Strabo as a guidebook.[6]

The collapse of the Ottoman authority brought about a more active Western presence. Venice briefly occupied the Morea and Vienna began pressing against the Danube. Towards the end of the seventeenth century we find the first accounts of the founding of Vlach villages, and in the eighteenth century these Vlach villages became rich through trading with new markets in the Austro-Hungarian Empire. It was in the eighteenth century that, with trade in mind, English settlers started setting up the British Empire and Russian settlers started expanding into Siberia. Vlach traders were doing the same kind of thing, with the important difference that they were not part of the Vlach Empire but of the Turkish, and the language they were helping to spread was not Vlach but Greek.[7]

The difficult inter-relationship between Vlach and Greek has never been satisfactorily explained. Greek was the language of the church, of education and of commerce. Vlach has never been a written language, there has never been a real Vlach church, and even Vlach's cousin Romanian, handicapped by a Slavonic alphabet, was slow to catch up with Greek as a language of communication. So too were Serbian and Bulgarian, and their churches and schools started well behind Greek equivalents. Many leaders of Bulgarian, Serbian and Albanian independence movements were educated in Greek schools. The Vlachs were almost entirely so educated, and somehow were never able to disentangle themselves from the Greek influence.

As travellers and traders the Vlachs were scattered all over the Balkan peninsula. They had links with Romania, and commercial interests in Austria and Hungary, but most of their bases were in the central southern part of the Balkans. They traded freely within and outside the Ottoman Empire. Though not a written language, as a spoken language Vlach was a good lingua franca. The absence of many Vlachs on voyages outside Vlach villages was good for the preservation of the language which mothers and grandmothers taught their children in the absence of their trading menfolk. Vlachs learnt loyalty to each other. The destruction by Ali Pasha of the great Vlach centre of Voskopojë at the end of the eighteenth century led to a greater Vlach presence being dispersed in other centres all over the Balkans.

The nineteenth century saw the rise of nationalism and the gradual disintegration of the Ottoman Empire in Europe into a number of small Balkan states. Until 1912, just within the memory of old Vlachs I have met, most Vlachs still lived within the Ottoman Empire, and there is a certain amount of evidence to show that they regretted its passing.[8] Travel was more difficult to practise across different tariff boundaries, transhumance was less easy when frontiers had to be crossed biannually. Unlike other nationalities the Vlachs had no written language and no national myth like Skanderbeg or Prince Lazar or Pericles to sustain them, and their earlier success in establishing themselves in scattered pockets throughout the Balkans meant that except in the northern Pindus mountains there was no compact body of Vlach-speakers to act as the nucleus of a Vlach state.

It was probably the last factor which was fatal to any idea of Vlach nationhood. Albania had similar sympathies towards the preservation of the Ottoman Empire and was very late in establishing an agreed alphabet.[9] But there was a compact body of Albanian-speakers, even if not all this body was included in the Albanian state created after the Balkan wars and recreated after the First World War. A Vlach state in the Pindus mountains was never a feasible proposition, and it was small wonder that Vlachs allied themselves to either Greeks or Romanians.

A remarkable picture of Vlachs just before the Balkan wars is presented by Wace and Thompson in *Nomads of the Balkans*.[10] Though travelling in difficult circumstances and largely based in Samarina, Greece, to which their classical training had drawn them, Wace and Thompson give a full and dispassionate account of Vlach villages throughout the Balkans. I found their map and that of the German student of the Balkans, G. Weigand, invaluable in tracing Vlach villages in the 1970s. Unlike Weigand and like Wace and Thompson, I did most of my work in Greece, to which I was drawn by a similar classical training and political circumstances. Rather to my surprise I found Vlach still spoken in most of the villages which first Weigand and then Wace and Thompson had visited. Admittedly in some of the villages only the old spoke the language, and admittedly most of the villages were but a shadow of their former glory. Nevertheless Vlach was still just about alive in the 1970s in Greece, preserved against all the odds by the innate conservatism of the people, still practising a kind of transhumance, deserting the mountain villages in winter, still tending to marry within the village or neighbourhood, and still a male-dominated society allowing children to be brought up by their Vlach-speaking mothers or grandmothers. I found little consciousness of being Vlach; people thought of themselves as Greeks speaking a strange kind of dialect. Minority rights did not seem very important twenty years

ago. The official Greek academic line was that the Vlachs
were descendants of Greek women who had married Roman soldiers, and this improbable theory was that adopted
by the Vlachs themselves if they showed any interest in
the subject.[11]

When I published *The Vlachs* in 1987 I came into contact
with other Vlach groups all over the world. Almost simultaneously the political complexion of the Balkans began to
change, and countries hitherto hard to visit opened their
doors to researchers, while others became suddenly
barred. I remember a three-week journey in 1988 where I
caught a bus from Dubrovnik to Sarajevo via Mostar,
visited without any difficulty the religious sites of Kosovo,
but had to look longingly at the high mountains of Albania.
The visit to Dubrovnik was occasioned by a conference on
non-dominant ethnic groups in Europe. Here I put forward
the thesis, based on researches in Greece, that Vlach was
strongest and the Vlach villages the most prosperous
where there had been least consciousness of the Vlachs as
being a separate people.[12]

This thesis was strengthened by my work on the Vlach
diaspora. Both in Romania and America I found a large
number of people who had emigrated from Greece because
as members of the pro-Romanian faction described by
Wace and Thompson they had found life difficult. They had
come from villages, now much reduced in size, where Vlach
no longer flourished. Pro-Greek centres like Metsovo continued to prosper, and the Vlach language was reasonably
strong in them.

As with the American Irish, the emigré is often more
vehement in support of his group than the people back in
the homeland. Emigré groups of Vlachs form societies, sing
sentimental songs – and occasionally indulge in theories
that are both fatuous and fascist about their racial origins.
As the Illyrians are seen as the ancestors of the Albanians,

so too the Vlachs like to regard themselves as the descendants of the original inhabitants of the central Balkans, although they can't quite decide who these inhabitants were. The Macedonians in spite of difficulties about this particular name seem promising; Alexander the Great is a useful ancestor to have. Alternatively, since Albanians have claimed the Illyrians, so the Vlachs have seized on the Thracians. Another tribe living north of Greece in Classical times were the Dardanians; indeed Dardania has been suggested as a less controversial name for the former Yugoslav province of Macedonia. Dardanians were an alternative title for Trojans; Aeneas, at any rate in Virgil, spoke Latin, and so really the Vlachs are Trojan. Quod erat demonstrandum.

These extraordinary theories and the old-fashioned racial philosophy that goes with them do not seem to be leading anywhere. The future of Vlach is uncertain, but it will be weakened, not strengthened, by fascist fantasies. In *The Vlachs* and in the first chapter of this book I do not predict a very strong or long future for the Vlach language. Strong communities in Romania, Albania and America may make these predictions a little premature, and I am glad to make this belated apology to my favourite fragment. The next three chapters inevitably have an autobiographical if not a journalistic air, but they are an attempt to correct and add to some of the historical facts of my earlier book.[13]

3

The Vlach Diaspora

By publishing a book on the Vlachs in English I inevitably came across English-speaking Vlachs in America and Australia. There is a Vlach society based on Freiburg in Germany; this occasionally holds conferences engendering rather more heat than light, but does provide useful arenas of communication for Vlachs throughout the world, and it was through their magazine *Zborlu Nostru* that I learnt about the Vlachs of Australia.

I arrived in Australia on March 30th and left on April 7th 1990. In this time I attended a Vlach funeral ceremony which replaced a dance, spoke about the Vlachs on Australian radio, gave a lecture at Melbourne University and spent some time with the Ministry of Ethnic Affairs in Melbourne. I also had several valuable conversations with Vlachs in Melbourne, whose kindness, hospitality and readiness to talk to me was almost overwhelming.

The Vlach Association of Australia was founded about eleven years ago on the initiative of some individuals from the Yugoslav Vlach village of Nižepolje. In the 1950s about five inhabitants from this village came to Melbourne and in the 1960s with greater relaxation from the Tito government their families and other villagers followed them. They formed a football team, kept closely together in two suburbs of Melbourne, Coburg and Keilor Park, and continued to speak their language, even bringing up their children born in Australia to speak Vlach. About 400 people would have attended the dinner dance. Most of these would have been from Nižepolje. Some would have been guests. A few would have been from other Vlach villages, but not many. Of the other Vlach villages near Nižepolje, Magarevo and Trnovo lost most of their population in Balkan migrations between the wars, and many of those from Gopeš and Malovište have moved to Sydney, not Melbourne. In Melbourne there is an association from Malovište, but this takes a Macedonian rather than a Vlach standpoint. There are many Greek Vlachs in Melbourne, but almost none bring up their children to speak Vlach, allying themselves with the large and powerful Greek community in Melbourne, not even distinguishing themselves as a subsection of this community as do the Cypriot and Pontic Greeks.

Nižepolje is in Yugoslav Macedonia, and it may seem surprising that the Australian government, which has agreed to a multi-cultural society, should carry its tolerance to the extent of allowing a Vlach association as well as a variety of separate associations for Croats, Serbs, Yugoslavs and Macedonians. The Australian Macedonians have had certain difficulties with the Greeks, probably as a result of external pressure, the name Macedonia and the presence of several Slav speakers in Greece being the causes of strife. In the cemetery tombstones in the Cyrillic and Greek alphabets stand side by side. There is also one inscription in Vlach. This lonely tomb is a good symbol of the difficulty Vlachs have in separating themselves from a Greek or Slav Macedonian identity, but also of their determination to do so.

It must be stressed that this determination has no political goal. There are associations in Victoria listed in the directory of Ethnic Community Affairs entitled Central Organizing Committee for Macedonian Human Rights in Aegean Macedonia and Pan Macedonian Association of Melbourne and Victoria. These seem to have a

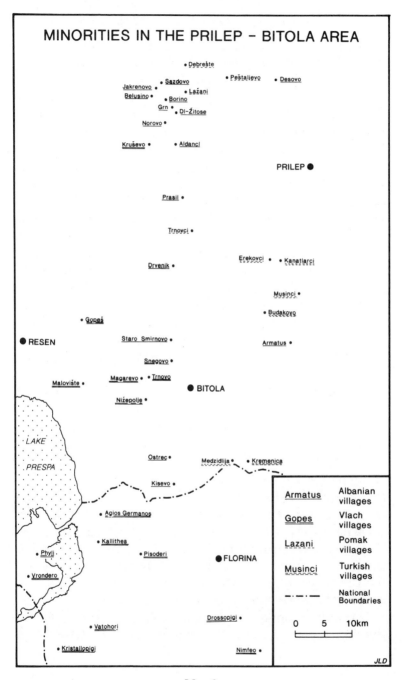

Map 3

slightly sinister purpose. The Vlachs only desire to preserve their language, their culture and their identity.

Even this may be difficult. I did meet two families of
Greek Vlachs who were sympathetic to the aims of the
Vlach association. One involved an enterprising pair of
young brothers from Aryiropoulion, a Vlach village near
Tirnavos in Thessaly.[1] They had arrived in Melbourne in
their teens, had obtained high qualifications in engineer-
ing, but had now set up a farm for Greek cheese with their
father and had plans for building a kind of Vlach craft
museum. But one had married a Greek, one a Jewish wife.
Another nice old man had actually attended a Romanian
school in Veroia and seemed extremely interested in Vlach
history. But his son spoke no Vlach and was just about to
marry a Greek girl, whose father from Crete gave me a
long lecture on how the Macedonians, Vlachs and Albanians were all really Greeks. Other Vlachs had naturally
married Australians and their children had grown up not
speaking Vlach, though they were kept vaguely interested
in the subject by the interest of one of their parents.

This kind of pattern seems to be more like the pattern
of interest in Vlach matters shown in America. Here there
are more Vlachs, but less encouragement from the United
States government to keep up languages other than English. Emigration to America from the Balkans has been
going on for a much longer time than emigration to Australia, and there has thus been more time for Vlachs to lose
their language. It might seem that Nižepolje Vlachs had
little hope for the future, although cooperation with other
Yugoslav Vlach communities in Sydney, tactful feelers to
the Greek Vlach community in Melbourne and even attempts to keep in touch with other Vlach associations
around the world would all be helpful moves.

Nor can we ignore the extraordinary resilience of the
five Vlach communities of Mount Pelister. In 1898 there

were over ten thousand inhabitants of the five villages, now there are barely a thousand. In 1898 they were overwhelmingly recorded as Vlach with the exception of the smallest, Nižepolje, whereas now Nižepolje is much the largest and the most Vlach. In view of Balkan wars, world wars, civil wars, and what is called progress, whereby dual carriageways replace mule tracks, high-rise flats replace peasant huts, and 1984 makes 1914 a nostalgic dream, such a survival seems remarkable, and my poetic analogy comparing the summer snow above the lake on the mountains overlooking Nižepolje to the survival of the Vlachs seems relatively accurate.[2]

I made discoveries in Australia about exactly what had happened to these villages. In 1912 they were still under Ottoman rule, passing briefly to Serbia as a result of the Balkan wars. The First World War meant that all the villages but Nižepolje passed under German-Bulgarian control while the French were in Nižepolje. This village was evacuated with the villagers passing to Katerini in Greece while from Magarevo many villagers were exiled to Bulgaria. The peace treaty brought Pelister back under Serbian rule, Serbia now being enlarged into Yugoslavia, and some of the villagers returned, although there was a great deal of emigration from all five villages to America, and some to Romania. The Second World War brought back the Germans and the Bulgarians, with Gopeš however being a partisan stronghold and the area to the west of Malovište being briefly under Italian-Albanian control. In 1945 Mount Pelister again formed part of Yugoslavia, this time great stress being laid on the Macedonian nature of the country. In schools the language of instruction has been changed from Serbian to Bulgarian, to Serbian, to Bulgarian, and then to Macedonian. Before 1912 the inhabitants of Pelister had the choice of a Bulgarian or Romanian or Greek school and, just to confuse the picture still further, there are Albanian speakers on Mount Pelister in Nižepolje and elsewhere.[3]

I met in Australia an interesting family whom I will call Babo, although their name has at various times been officially changed to Babović (Serb), Babov (Bulgarian) and Babovski (Macedonian). In Nižepolje in 1990 I met an old lady from this family born in 1900 who was educated at a Greek school and still speaks Greek. This devotion to the Greek cause is understandable in view of the way her Greek prayers have been so often answered. In the First World War her future husband, then called Babović, served in the Serbian army, but was wounded and taken prisoner, spending most of the war in Sopron, Hungary. On his return he found Nižepolje deserted with his own family in Katerini and his fiancée's family, who lived in Magarevo, somewhere in Bulgaria, but he found them both. In the Second World War one of their sons was called up by the Bulgarian army, and fought for them until they surrendered, whereupon dodging the partisans he fled to Greece, from which after some difficulties he emerged to be one of the pioneer Nižepolje settlers in Melbourne. His family became unpopular and had to endure another exile, this time to Delčevo on the Yugoslav-Bulgarian border. They returned from this, but another son was not happy and fled across the mountains to Greece, where the first person to greet him was a Vlach shepherd. He then joined his brother in Australia. With a relaxation of the political atmosphere in Yugoslavia good communications have been established. The old lady has visited Australia for an operation, the Australian exiles have visited Nižepolje, and younger members of the family have emigrated to Melbourne. Two brothers still live in Yugoslavia. One was visiting Melbourne while I was there. Jim Babo, born in Australia, son of the Bulgarian soldier, is treasurer of the Vlach association and obviously an extremely successful chartered accountant. End of an everyday story of Vlach country folk.

In America, arriving on April 7th and leaving on April 18th, I visited Vlach communities in New York and Bridge-port, Connecticut under the auspices of the Society Far-sarotul[4] and on my own initiative went to see two Vlachs with whom I had been in correspondence in Los Angeles and Washington. In Los Angeles I met the famous John Zdru, recently expelled from Greece, presumably for pub-lishing a Vlach newspaper in America.[5] He was with two younger men, whose families had originated in Albania and Petrič, Bulgaria, but had then moved to Romania. In Washington I met Dr Socrates Asteriou who had taught history at university level and worked on the Balkans at the State Department. He had been born in the United States shortly after his parents had moved from Trnovo, Yugoslavia, at the end of the First World War. His mother had been a member of the pro-Greek upper bourgeoisie in that town and his father had worked for the Turkish administration. He had only recently become aware of his Vlach origins, a phenomenon very common among Greek-speaking Vlachs who have emigrated. In Bridgeport and New York this phenomenon was less apparent, for the very good reason that most members of the Society Farsarotul came from an area where little or no Greek was spoken. This was the area around Korçë in Albania. Many had lived in the villages of Pljasë, now deserted, and Dishnicë. The village of Shipckë and town of Bilisht were also men-tioned. There was talk of Voskopojë, generally agreed to have suffered badly in both wars. There are still Vlach-speakers in this area, and in the month when I was visiting many telephone calls had been received from relatives in Albania.[6]

The pro-Romanian sympathies of the group were easily apparent. Most of the elderly people to whom I spoke had attended a Romanian school, paid for by the Romanian government. Some remembered a Greek priest being killed in Pljasë and a Greek bishop in Korçë having his nose and beard pulled by indignant Vlachs. Many were related to Haralambu Balamaci, a Vlach killed by the Greeks. The Romanian schools had been conducted in Romanian, which the Vlachs had found difficult but not impossible to understand. I learnt from them a good deal of Romanian nationalism and inaccurate ancient history. Calling themselves incorrectly and confusingly Macedonians, the Vlachs of Albania seemed to regard Alexander the Great as one of themselves, and I heard two old men refer to the Battle of Pharsalia as an explanation for the name Farsherot. Almost without exception, the Bridgeport and New York Vlachs spoke ill of the Greeks and well of the Turks. Most spoke a little Albanian, but they had had little experience of Albanian rule. One man spoke kindly of King Zog.

The Society Farsarotul had been founded in 1903 originally as a means of providing a proper funeral for its members. In the early part of this century many young men had come over to work in the woollen mills of New England. Some of these men had returned to find a bride and then left for America again. Usually the marriages were arranged. One heard rather harrowing stories of young women marrying men they had never met, or visiting America at a tender age to meet brothers or even fathers they had scarcely seen.

The Balkan wars of 1912 and the subsequent occupation during the First World War of southern Albania by Greek and then Italian and French forces had increased the rate of emigration. The Romanian schools had closed, although they had reopened after the war. Most of the people I spoke to had been involved with sheep or transporting goods by mules. Some had been genuine transhumants, travelling

to Sesklo, Almiro or Aryiropoulion in southern Thessaly
during the winter, although in most cases the women had
stayed in Albania. I met one old lady with vivid memories
of the journey, which involved silencing the bells of the
sheep as they passed by Ioannina. This lady spoke rather
more kindly of the Greeks. The erection of new frontiers
after the Balkan wars had done great damage to transhumant shepherds and to merchants transporting goods by
mule. Insufficient winter grazing and the harsh climate
near Korçë had wreaked havoc on large herds.

In 1925 the Romanian government had offered new land
in the southern Dobrudja to the Albanian Vlachs. Many
had seized the opportunity. Pljasë had been virtually
abandoned, and the school closed. A new settlement had
been made in the Dobrudjan town of Frashati, but unfortunately in 1940 this area had reverted to Bulgaria, forcing
the Vlachs to move once again. Some had emigrated in or
after the war to America, others had moved or been moved
to other areas in Romania. One family said that the Communist authorities had given them and other Vlach families two hours' notice to move from Timisoara to
somewhere near the Russian border. Rather surprisingly
these experiences did not seem to have diminished either
pro-Romanian sentiments or the feeling that the Vlachs
were slightly different, speaking a different language and
tending to marry among themselves. Most of the emigrants to the United States would arrive speaking little or
no English, and they would arrive to join a close-knit
community where almost everybody was related to everybody else. This helped the preservation of the language,
but only for a time. The shock of arriving at a school
speaking no English was sufficient to persuade many
Vlachs born between the wars not to repeat the experiment
of speaking only Vlach to their children. Hence Vlachs of
the third generation are not speaking their language,

although a few are moved by curiosity to take an interest in the subject. Moreover Vlachs are now marrying outside their race; although the custom of going back to the old country for a wife died hard, neither the Albanian nor the Romanian governments favoured such romances. Oddly, many Vlachs in America had visited both Albania and Romania, and Vlachs from Romania were still escaping from the country. Recent events in Romania may increase the supply of Vlach-speakers in America, but there is clearly something of a crisis among the Vlach community, reflected by tensions within the Society Farsarotul.[7]

There are many Vlachs in America who do not come from either Albania or Romania, but as in Australia most of these have attached themselves to the much larger Greek community. The orthodox community in America, some six and a half million strong, is divided into two sections. The Greek orthodox churches conduct their services in Greek, and with a large number of post-war immigrants this is understandable. Other orthodox churches, Russian, Serb, Albanian and Romanian, have services mainly in English. On Easter Sunday the Romanian priest in Fairfield, near Bridgeport announced that Christ was risen in English, Vlach, Romanian and Greek, but he spoke mainly in English with a brief Romanian précis of his sermon. This pattern would not be repeated in Greek churches. Thus religion is a divisive factor.

Efforts to reach out to the Greek Vlach community are handicapped by the reluctance of such Vlachs to admit their identity and by the hostility some members of the Society Farsarotul feel for anything that is Greek. There are Greek members of the Society, but they come from the pro-Romanian sector that persisted in Greece between the wars when Romanian-financed schools still survived. I talked to the mother of the secretary of the Society who had taught in Avdella, Mr Zdru's brother who had taught in Kedronas, and Mr Zdru's sister-in-law whose father had taught in Paticina, erroneously transcribed as Patima in *The Vlachs*.[8] The subject was clearly a delicate one. There had been hostility from the Greeks and a certain amount of fraternization with the Latin-speaking Italians. Fearful of arousing unhappy memories, I did not probe too deeply into the war years or the even more difficult civil war. I did learn that the schools went on until 1944, although the Romanians had stopped paying salaries after 1942. There had been a secondary and commercial school in Salonica, and some training for teachers had been provided in Bucharest.

Such Romanian teachers would both foster and be fostered by the pro-Romanian stance held by some members of the Society Farsarotul. It is however possible to exaggerate this stance. Mr Zdru fought loyally in the Greek army. In a newsletter of the society there is a touching account by a Mr Tega of how, while in the American army in 1945, he had visited relatives in Flambourarion and Vovousa.[9] I found no Vlach-speakers in Flambourarion. Mr Tega was luckier, and he was even luckier in Vovousa, scene of a great Greek victory over the Italians in 1940. His name was proudly displayed as a war hero, and he found his future wife among the Vlach villagers of Vovousa.

It is as well to inject this happier note, which also dispels the legend that the Vlachs were more guilty than most of collaborating with the enemy. On the contrary some Vlachs maintained that it was their villages that were singled out for the kind of savage destruction that befell Klisura. This seems a legend too. Clearly such legends do no good for the Vlach cause, which must reach out to Vlachs in other countries if it is to survive in America. Many of these Vlachs have ties with Greece, and an anti-

Greek approach from American Vlachs linked oddly to
Romania and Albania is counter-productive.

Some people in Bridgeport had relatives in Melbourne.
Vlach families from Albania had settled in Nižepolje, and
people from Nižepolje had gone to America as well as
Australia. The two communities could learn much from
each other's experiences, and the Society Farsarotul could
profit from an exchange of ideas. Of course there are
differences over and above the rather comic fact that
funerals provided the spur in America as opposed to football in Australia. The earlier attitude of the American
government to the learning of English and the drying up
of the sources of immigration in Albania and Romania
means that the language is in more danger in Bridgeport
than it is in Melbourne. In Melbourne the Vlachs are torn
between Macedonia and Greece; one hears practically
nothing of Albania or Romania. I gave a lecture in both
Australia and America, and in both places said that I
thought Alexander the Great was a Greek and that Justinian was a kind of Vlach. In Australia there were some
who claimed that Alexander was either a Vlach or a Slav,
while in America there were some who claimed that both
men were Illyrian Albanians.

The paradoxes continue. A common factor in both communities is their reluctance to associate or be associated
with the Greeks, even though such an association is desirable, but the reluctance is understandable. The Vlachs of
Mount Pelister and southern Albania have never lived
under Greek rule, except in the exceptional circumstances
of war, and have learnt little Greek. In contrast most
Greek Vlachs were born in what is now Greece and speak
Greek perhaps more easily than they speak Vlach. It will
be hard to bring scattered sections of the community
together, perhaps harder in closely connected suburbs of
Melbourne or Bridgeport than in those villages of the

Balkans which were once united by mule tracks but are now separated by national frontiers. The threat is different in different areas, and perhaps the best way to defeat it is for these different areas to meet and share their experiences.

Since 1990 I have kept in touch with both the communities of Bridgeport and Melbourne. In 1991 I met up with my Melbourne hosts in Bitola; there were twenty dinars to the pound, and I had travelled in a train from Slovenia to Macedonia.[10] Events in the former Yugoslavia have cast a tragic shadow over the Macedonian immigrants to Melbourne, although strangely there have been odd recrudescences of Vlach nationalism in the new Macedonia uneasily pitched between Greece and Serbia, scarcely recognised by either, with a large Albanian population and other odd fragments as well, Turks, Pomaks, Bulgarians and Serbs. There even seem signs that Macedonia will do something for Vlach rights in the same way as a bankrupt facing huge debts pays the milkman.

In contrast the Bridgeport Vlach community is now in contact with relations and friends in Albania and Romania. They have visited Vlach villages in both countries, although inevitably there is a huge gap between the culture of suburban America and the Balkan villages. I too have been invited to visit homes which would have been difficult if not impossible to see in 1987, and I record these visits in the next two chapters.

Vlachs in Albania

I had visited Albania three times before the Communist regime fell, in organised tours which allowed little freedom of movement or opportunity to see Vlachs. My experiences in America and the gradual opening up of Albania to individual travel prompted me to make two more visits in 1992 and 1993. These visits made it clear that my earlier estimates of the number of Vlachs was too low, and I am anxious to correct this impression. Much more work could and should be done among these Vlachs, preserved by the harshness of Hoxha from the corrupting effects of modern civilisation.

The timing of my first visit, between March 20th and March 26th 1992, was not exactly fortunate. After a winter of discontent Albania had a general election on March 21st. These elections were introduced to resolve the problems of unemployment, inflation, mass emigration, poverty and despair, of which we saw ample evidence in the untilled fields and dingy towns. We saw little evidence of famine or violence, of which we had heard much, but we were perhaps fortunate in being in the south of the country, where there is more aid from Greece and Italy, both directly from these governments, and indirectly through people working there. A strong police presence was observable in election week, when we were frequently and perhaps fortunately mistaken for friendly foreign delegations, instead of enquiring historians.

We crossed the border on March 20th at Kapenitsa and

were driven to Korçë, a city with quite a large Vlach population, some of whom we met. That same evening we went to Boboshticë, a Vlach village, where the very helpful president of the local Vlach association lived. Here we were treated to traditional Vlach hospitality, and I could not help being reminded of a similar arrival in the Vlach community of Melbourne in March 1990. There were the same friendliness, food, open doors, pressing hospitality, jokes, toasts, speeches and singing. But there were differences. Australia has always been free, Albania almost never. It was warm in the Melbourne autumn, near freezing in the Albanian spring.

Boboshticë is an interesting Vlach community. Earlier visitors, notably the great Weigand, have commented on a Bulgarian minority here, and there is a linguistic account of this minority before the Second World War.[1] I asked about this minority, and got a dusty answer. There were two churches in this village, and we were shown one. It had magnificent paintings dating from the seventeenth century. We were told that the other church was Byzantine. The church we saw was dedicated to St John. When I asked innocently whether this meant the Baptist or the Evangelist, I received a long lecture on Orthodoxy as opposed to the Baptist or Evangelist church. Enver Hoxha, like Big Brother, has almost wiped out the past, so that saints and churches are almost unknown. This was a difficulty in enquiring about history. Another obvious difficulty was that our jolly hosts at Boboshticë were naturally more interested in asking us questions about our present than in answering questions about their past.[2]

We returned to Korçë and next day set out to Voskopojë, a famous, if not *the* famous, city in Vlach history, a city I had been determined to see since 1974. Our entry was unpropitious. The road was bad and became worse. We slid

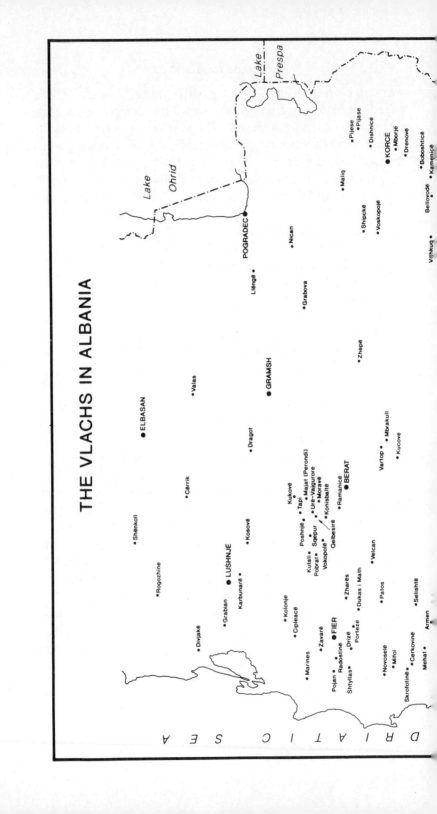

THE VLACHS IN ALBANIA

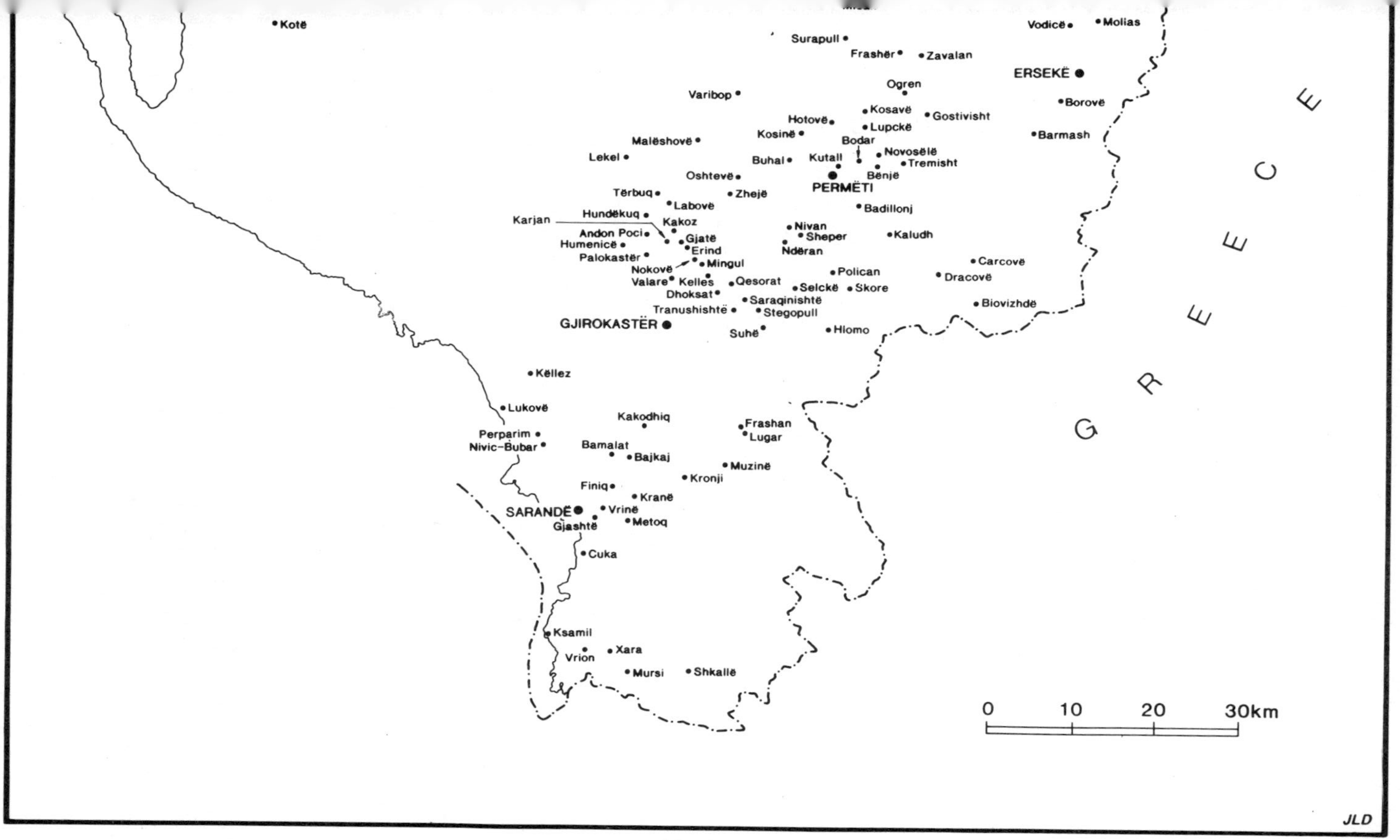

Kotë

Vodicë • •Molias

ERSEKË ●
•Borovë
•Barmash

Surapull• Frashër• •Zavalan
Ogren• •Gostivisht
•Kosavë •Lupckë
Varibop• Hotovë• Bodar •Novoselë
Kosinë• Kutall •Tremisht
Maleshovë• Buhal• PËRMETI •Carcovë
Lekel• Oshtevë• •Zhejë •Badilonj
•Labovë •Nivan •Kaludh
Terbuq• Kakoz •Sheper •Dracovë
Andon Poçi •Glatë Ndëran •Polican •Biovizhde
Karjan Humenicë• •Erind Qesorat •Selckë •Skore
Hundëkuq •Mingul Kellës •Saraqinishtë
Palokaster• Nokovë• Dhoksat• •Stegopull
Valare• Tranushishtë •Hlomo
GJIROKASTER ● Suhë•

•Këllez •Frashan
Kakodhiq •Lugar
Lukovë• Bamalat• •Muzinë
Perparim •Bajkaj
Nivic–Bubar• Finiq• •Kronji
Kranë•
SARANDË● •Vrinë
Gjashtë• •Metoq
•Cuka
•Ksamil •Xara
Vrion •Mursi •Shkallë

G R E E C E

0   10   20   30km

Map 4

JLD

in the snow into what looked like a poor mean mountain village, although our welcome was overwhelming.

Voskopojë, formerly Moschopolis, was a flourishing community in the eighteenth century with a multitude of churches, and, though there still seems doubt about this, an academy and a printing press. Ali Pasha destroyed this community in a series of wars at the end of the eighteenth century, and citizens from Voskopojë reinforced Vlach communities all over the Balkans. Nevertheless the population of this area remained basically Vlach, and Weigand gave quite an encouraging account of the state of the village at the end of the nineteenth century. It suffered further in the First World War, but we heard happy accounts from present inhabitants of how between the wars the six surviving churches were visited each day in Holy week. Now there are only three churches which survive in a recognisable condition from some number like thirty-seven. We saw two of these, St Nicholas and St Athanasius, battered, bedaubed with vulgar graffiti, but still magnificent. There are also traces in Voskopojë's wide streets of its great past, and it seems tragic that more cannot be done for what seems an obvious centre of Vlach history, although both Greek and Albanian historians would dispute this.[3]

From Voskopojë we proceeded to Tirana where our escort, Mr Shituni, and our two taxi drivers were anxious to vote in the elections. I met various members of the Vlach community in Tirana and, had it not been for the elections, would have attended a meeting of Vlachs in Albania. I also met the Romanian Ambassador who seemed interested in the Vlachs.

We then passed to Selenicë, a small town well to the south of Tirana. The journey took a long time. Roads are bad. We were rapturously received. Selenicë has attracted a certain amount of attention from historians on account of its mines which appear to go back to antiquity.[4] Nobody, however, has mentioned that it is primarily a Vlach town with a strong Vlach consciousness. We were told that about three out of four of its five thousand inhabitants spoke Vlach, and this seemed not a totally idle boast. The ruined church had a Greek dedication and a modern Romanian icon. The inhabitants claimed that it had been built in the seventeenth century and the houses in the eighteenth. Our wonderful hosts, who put us up in the best bedrooms, while they slept in nooks and crannies, did give some insight into how the language had been preserved. A family unit is considered to be one of three generations, all living in the same house or apartment. The parents are all expected to work long hours, leaving the children to be brought up by the grandparents who speak Vlach to them, even if one of the parents is not a Vlach-speaker.

From Selenicë we proceeded via Tepelenë, Ali Pasha's capital, to Andon Poçi, the home village of Mr Shituni, where we spent two nights. This village had been mentioned to me as a Vlach village on my first visit to Albania in 1976, and gets a mention, wrongly spelt, in my book on the Vlachs.[5] In 1963 Vlachs formerly living in rude huts had been settled in this village, full of quite handsome houses, built in three straight rows. The village seemed relatively prosperous, but this prosperity may have been an illusion, resulting from wealth brought in by young men who had emigrated to Greece. As so often when arriving in a Vlach village one was met by the very old and the very young. Some of the former spoke Greek and remembered the days when they and their flocks had moved freely across the border. The very young spoke Vlach without embarrassment. Greek, Albanian and Vlach in this area are hard to disentangle, and recent political events make the task harder, since people anxious to emigrate to Greece are naturally anxious to claim Greek relatives and the Greek language.

From Andon Poçi I made a long drive with Mr Shituni to a Vlach conference in Lushnjë, a quite large but not particularly distinguished town, north of Fier and Vlorë on the coastal plain where earlier historians of the Vlachs like Weigand and Wace and Thompson had recorded a strong Vlach presence. The conference at Lushnjë proved the point of these historians. There was an audience of about three hundred people. It is true that after speeches in Vlach and Albanian, it was decided to use Albanian. My speech in Vlach, Albanian and English was received kindly. I enquired where people had come from, and was told that they had mainly come from Lushnjë, although the village of Karbunarë near Fier was also mentioned. Weigand mentions a number of villages in the coastal plain, but, given transport difficulties in Albania, I doubt if many of these villagers made it to the conference. Our taxi broke down, and I had to hitch a lift in a lorry.[6]

From Lushnjë we returned to Andon Poçi. The road to this village is a rough one, just negotiable by car; Vlach villages further up the mountains would need special transport. We had planned a long journey to Kapenitsa via the road, built by the Italians, running along Albania's southern border, but the track to Andon Poçi had damaged one of the cars, and we had to take the short road to Kakavia. Here there was a scrum of Albanians trying to get into Greece, through which we had to pass, alternately waving our British passports in polite fashion and adopting rough tactics that I had learnt when playing the Eton wall game. There was not much time during these manoeuvres to take linguistic notes on the composition of the scrum, but in the bus to Ioannina I heard more Greek than Albanian, and I also heard some Vlach.

My book on the Vlachs was treated with great respect

in Albania. This respect was undeserved as much of what I had written in this book was clearly incorrect. In particular I had underestimated the number of Vlachs in Albania together with the total number of Vlachs in the Balkans. This latter number I calculated as no more that fifty thousand, using Wace and Thompson's 1914 figure of 500,000 and dividing it by ten after comparing the number of Vlach-speakers in certain areas then and now. Thus the five Vlach villages of Mount Pelister near Bitola in Yugoslavia have now only a thousand inhabitants between them, as opposed to ten thousand before the First World War. This is partly because people have left the villages for the towns, and I found quite a few Vlachs in high-rise flats in Skopje and Bitola. It is of course these Vlachs who tend to lose their language, but in Albania harsh social conditions in cramped living quarters have, as I saw in Selenicë, kept the language going among children.

In addition emigration which led many Yugoslavs to leave for Australia after the war has not been possible until very recently for Albanians, although there were emigrations between the wars to Romania and the United States. My experience at Lushnjë suggested quite a large Vlach presence in the towns, although the language was not spoken by everyone. Fier, Vlorë, Korçë, Elbasan and Tirana were mentioned as towns with a considerable Vlach population. Enver Hoxha can be credited with raising the birth rate and reducing infant mortality, and Vlachs are more likely to survive in houses at Andon Poçi than in huts. All these factors point to an increase in the number of Vlachs. The Vlach association now has twenty thousand members and they claim that they are a bigger minority than the Slavs or even the Greeks.[7]

In addition to the towns there are a number of other areas where Vlachs are to be found in greater quantities than has been allowed for by previous writers. Wace and

Thompson did not visit the coastal plain near Fier, and Weigand's visit was a brief one, although they both correctly said there were Vlachs there. These they assumed to be Vlachs coming down from the mountains in the winter in the same way as Vlachs in the Pindus mountains, or even in some cases from eastern Albania, used to winter their flocks in the Thessalian plain. Transhumance makes counting numbers very difficult, since one is liable to count the Vlachs twice or not at all. Neither Weigand nor Wace and Thompson noted Selenicë, too large a settlement to count as a mere winter camp, and the proximity of the Vlach settlements to Apollonia and the beginning of the Via Egnatia leads to the possibility, suggested by Hammond, that this area has always been a reservoir of Latin speech, from which the Vlachs expanded.[8] More work needs to be done on the villages and towns of this area. My historical enquiries rarely got back further than the seventeenth century, as is the case also with Vlach settlements in Greece.

In addition to the coastal plains I noted four other areas of Vlach settlement. First there are a number of villages in the Korce area, Llengë, Shipckë, Dishnicë, Boboshticë, Borovë and Pljasë. These are the villages from which the Farsherot community in Bridgeport, Connecticut sprang, and they have a distinct identity. Voskopojë is in this area, but has rather a different history. Then there are the Vlachs in the Grammos mountains adjoining the Greek border, and reached with difficulty off the road we did not take. There was widespread emigration from both these areas to Romania as well as to America, and in Romania I heard how the Gramoshteani had retained their identity and speech less successfully than the Farsheroti. Then there are the Vlachs intermingled with Greeks in the two main areas of Greek speech in Albania, so well described by Hammond, the villages along the coast as far north as

Himarë, and the villages along the Drin valley near Gjirokastër. Andon Poçi is one purely Vlach village in the latter category, Shkallë near Sarandë in the former. As in the villages in Greece near Igoumenitsa, villages which I have never visited and which I overlooked in writing *The Vlachs*, Albanian, Greek and Vlach are very confused in this part of the world, and the political events of the last fifty years have hardly resolved the confusion.[9]

The political events of the last years offer a unique opportunity to study the Vlachs as nobody else has studied them. Albania is a country which faces so many difficulties that the Vlachs may seem unimportant. Albania's two closest neighbours, Greece and the former Yugoslavia, reveal all too clearly the dangers of minorities in any state. Greece, which tends to deny that it has minorities, would seem to have done better than Yugoslavia, whose minorities are tearing it apart. Some of the Vlachs of Albania who prefer to call themselves Aroumanians seemed to look to Romania as a source of help, confusing Cinderella with the Fairy Godmother. It is certainly interesting that the congress at Lushnjë took this line, and the people in this northern area do a great deal to contradict the common equation of Vlachs with Greeks. It would clearly be impertinent to give political advice to the Vlachs of Albania on how to conduct their own future. All that Vlachs in other countries and friends of Vlachs in all countries can do is to provide material support in helping them to preserve and restore their heritage, and intellectual support in helping them to find out what their heritage is. At Lushnjë, as at so many Vlach conferences, I heard heady talk of the long and distinguished ancestry of the Vlachs, and this is clearly a mistake, as indeed is the kind of nationalism that requires a national myth. But everyone has the right to find out about his or her own history. The history of the Vlachs in Albania is both so interesting and so unknown that we must make every effort to help them discover their true identity.

In 1993 I visited Albania again in July. This time we crossed over by boat from Corfu to Sarandë, hired a car at vast expense and drove where we liked. We went to see old friends at Selenicë and Voskopojë, saw some Greek villages in the south, found Vlachs at Ardenicë and Borovë, but shortage of time and poor roads meant that we saw only a few of the Vlach villages we had wished to visit. It was high summer and the coutryside looked more prosperous. Private enterprise has brought out a host of small cafés in the towns. But schools, hospitals and public services in general are sadly neglected, and the country is still losing its human seed corn, as young men and women leave to work abroad. This is particularly true of the Vlachs where there is a tradition of going abroad for work, and where Italy with its Latinate language and Greece with its fellow Vlachs seem close and attractive. I did use my second visit to find out more information about Vlach villages.

The map of the Vlach villages (pp. 58-9) was prepared from two lists sent to me by Mr Auron Kristo of Elbasan and Mr Misto Shunda of Tirana. The two lists were very different from each other, although I have no reason to doubt the good faith of their compilers, to whom I am very grateful. I have consulted large-scale maps of the Communist era and German staff maps before that era as well as maps made for special studies of the Vlachs in the Balkans, but have been unable to find a number of villages, and would welcome information about them.[10] For these omissions and any inaccuracies I am responsible. In two short visits to Albania I have been unable to visit any villages at length apart from Borovë, Boboshticë, Voskopojë,

Andon Poçi, Selenicë and Kolonjë, and am therefore rely-
ing on second-hand information.

Albania is divided into a number of provinces, named
after the chief town of the district. Almost inevitably
Vlachs will be found in such towns, marked in capital
letters in the map, although it is in such towns that Vlachs
tend to lose their identity and are hard to find. On the other
hand, it is among urban Vlachs that one very often finds
leaders of Vlach organisations. In Macedonia, after scour-
ing the villages only to find old people and young children,
I was pleased to find active Vlach-speakers in the high-rise
flats of Bitola and Skopje, and I think the same phenomenon can be found in Albania.

Inevitably this map will lead to questions about the
total number of Vlachs in Albania. Here there are a
number of difficulties. Exact numbers are very hard to
calculate at the moment owing to widespread emigration
to Greece and Italy. It is not easy to estimate the number
of Vlachs in towns. Even in villages there is a wide gap
between some which are totally Vlach and some which
only have one or two Vlach families. Thus in Voskopojë
I was told that Shengerj had only a few Vlachs, and
Shipckë no non-Vlachs. I could not find Shengerj on any
map, and could only find Shipckë in specialist Vlach
maps.

Then there is the problem of what constitutes a Vlach.
Is it someone who habitually speaks the language or someone who has a feeling of Vlach identity? The two are clearly
not synonymous. At Lushnjë in 1992 there was plenty of
Vlach fervour, but it was obvious fairly soon that proceedings would have to be conducted in Albanian. On the other
hand, I have met simple people in the countryside happily
speaking Vlach, but hardly aware that there was anything
special or strange in doing so. It is very difficult for an
outsider, speaking very little Vlach or Albanian, to test a

village's speech patterns. The villagers tend to adopt the speech of the interpreter, and I had a Vlach interpreter in 1992 and an Albanian interpreter in 1993. Greater freedom since 1992 has of course meant more liberty for Vlach-speakers to say and think what they like about their language; it has also meant greater mobility and the breaking up of all Vlach-speaking family and village units.

In Selenicë I made careful enquiries of Mr Nasha Dhamaj, a Vlach who had studied the problems of his race carefully. He estimated that there were about 12,000 Vlachs in the twelve villages named in the Vlorë province. If this estimate was used as a basis for a rough estimate for the hundred villages on my list we would come up with a hundred thousand Vlach villagers. To this we would probably have to add another hundred thousand for Vlachs in towns. A total of 200,000, though below that given by some optimistic Vlachs, is very much a maximum figure, including both those who think of themselves as Vlach but don't speak the language and those who speak the language but think of themselves as purely Albanian. Fifty thousand would be a rough figure for those who satisfy both criteria. Even this figure is much larger than the one I gave when writing *The Vlachs* in 1987.

I read in a respectable and responsible English newspaper that the 400,000 ethnic Greeks in Albania are a potential source of conflict in the area.[11] The Albanians play down this number and the conflict involved, and they are right to do so.[12] Albania is supposed to have a total population of three million, of whom fifteen per cent are orthodox. The Greeks have constantly confused orthodox religion with ethnic consciousness and it seems likely that the figure of 400,000 is a religious figure. My figures would suggest that about half this figure is taken up by Vlachs.

A few of these Vlachs in the south speak a little Greek.

Some have parents who were born in Greece during a transhumant migration. The Greeks have offered help in rebuilding Vlach churches, and with a strange mixture of hospitality and chauvinism have been generous in allowing Vlachs to work in Greece. In certain places near Sarande and near Gjirokastër, Vlachs and Greeks can be found in the same villages. In some areas near Himarë and the western bank of the Drin Greeks predominate. On the other hand, near Korçë and near Vlorë there is very little Greek spoken, and any Greek claims to these areas must rely entirely on the very different Vlachs.

Just where the Vlachs go now is a matter of uncertainty and concern. Unlike the genuine Greek-speakers in Albania, who have a powerful neighbour to assist them in obtaining educational rights, the Vlachs have only distant Romania, and Vlach, as well as being distinct from Romanian, is not as yet a written language. The Albanians claim that the Greeks do have educational rights, although I saw graffiti in Greek villages denouncing this claim. The Vlachs have received promises, but as yet no implementation. It is perhaps worth mentioning that neither Albanians nor Vlachs in Greece have any kind of rights. It is possible that, as in Greece, the Vlachs in Albania may succeed in preserving some kind of identity through a lack of aggression. The idea of being a loyal Albanian, though still being a Vlach, is not an unworthy one, shared by the American citizen proud of his Polish origins or the Englishman who supports Ireland at football.

One advantage the Vlachs do have as part of their heritage is the presence of many beautiful monuments in or near their villages. As well as the sorely battered but beautiful churches of Voskopojë and the gracefully restored church of Ardenicë I note on my maps a number of villages where a Vlach village contained a church sometimes marked as a monument worthy of note. After nearly fifty years first of disapproval of religion and then a total ban on it, it is difficult to calculate the state of these churches, but future investigators might make the villages with churches a priority in recreating the culture of the Vlachs of Albania.[13]

Vlachs in Romania

The relationship between Vlachs and Romanians is difficult to disentangle, more difficult to explain. In the absence of any mention of Latin-speakers in the Balkans either north or south of the Danube for nearly four hundred years after the collapse of the Danube frontier in 602 it is naturally difficult to decide at what stage Vlachs became distinct from Romanians. Even in the next five hundred years, when there are many mentions of Vlachs, and when there are the first references to Romanians, it is sometimes difficult to know which group is being referred to. For instance, did the Vlach-Bulgarian Asenid empire contain Vlachs and Bulgarians, or Romanians and Bulgarians, or all three? Linguists give various dates for the segregation of the two languages, or two dialects of the same language; the distinction between dialect and language is hard to make.

In the Ottoman period the distinction is blurred because many Vlachs from the southern Balkans crossed the Danube and either traded with or settled in Romania. Romania enjoyed a precarious semi-independence from Turkish rule, but its cultural level was not high, and up until the middle of the nineteenth century Vlachs seemed to be giving more to Romania than vice versa. The Vlach link with the Greeks was important as in the first half of the nineteenth century Romania was ruled by the Greek Phanariots, and we have the extraordinary phenomenon of the movement for Greek independence beginning with a revolt by Prince Hypsilanti in Romania.

In the second half of the nineteenth century Romania gained full independence and a monarch from the West. The Romanian language was subtly altered, so that words with French and Italian roots replaced Slavonic ones. Vlach did not have many Slavonic roots, but the two languages did become more separate. There were still confusions. Western travellers called Vlachs Wallachians, a clear reminder of a Romanian province. The name Aroumanian was as confusing. The Romanians, anxious for a hand in the Balkan stakes, began calling the Vlachs Macedo-Romanians. It was now the turn of the Vlachs living in the poverty-stricken war-ridden southern Balkans to be the country cousins, and we find Romania devoting large sums to the provision of Vlach schools.

Some of these Vlach schools survived until the Second World War, with the result that it is possible today to find people in Vlach villages speaking pure Romanian. The schools were, however, never particularly strong, and the pro-Romanian party was generally in a minority in most Balkan villages.[1] After the First World War many members of this minority party left for Romania. They left from Greece where schools survived but where they were particularly unpopular, from Bulgaria where they were a small minority but where population exchanges with Bulgarians in Romania were possible, and from Yugoslavia and Albania where there were no schools and widespread poverty. There was a somewhat artificial Vlach literary movement fostered by Romania.[2]

Romania had been on the winning side in both the second Balkan war and the First World War, and, though her fighting record had not been particularly distinguished in either struggle, she had been rewarded with large areas containing a non-Romanian population. In

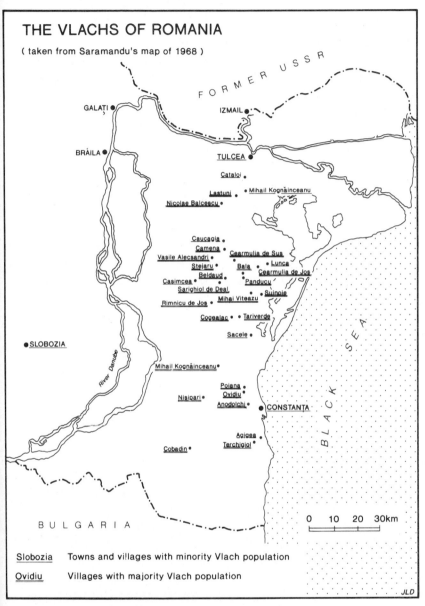

THE VLACHS OF ROMANIA

(taken from Saramandu's map of 1968)

FORMER USSR

GALAȚI ●

IZMAIL ●

BRĂILA ●

TULCEA ●

Cataloi ●

Lastuni ●   ● Mihail Kogniăinceanu

Nicolae Balcescu ●

Caucagia ●

Camena ●   ● Cearmulia de Sus

Vasile Alecsandri ●   ● Lunca

Stejaru ●   Bala ●   Cearmulia de Jos

Beldaud ●   ● Panducu

Casimcea ●

Sarighiol de Deal ●   ● Suinoie

Rimnicu de Jos ●   Mihai Viteazu ●

Cogealac ●   ● Tariverde

Sacele ●

● SLOBOZIA

River Danube

Mihail Kogniăinceanu ●

Poiana ●

Nisipari ●   Ovidiu ●

Anodolchi ●   ● CONSTANȚA

BLACK SEA

Agigea ●

Cobadin ●   Techigiol ●

BULGARIA

0   10   20   30km

Slobozia   Towns and villages with minority Vlach population

Ovidiu   Villages with majority Vlach population

JLD

Map 5

1913 she had been awarded the southern Dobrudja at the expense of Bulgaria, but in 1918 after the Romanian defeat at the hands of the Germans Bulgaria was awarded the whole of the Dobrudja, which however reverted to Romania in 1919. It was in this strange delta of the Danube, surrounded by rivers but containing surprisingly high hills, that most of the Vlachs settled or were settled. It was a sensible place to which to move a basically Latin-speaking population, being like the Banat in the south-western part of the country a mosaic of different ethnic groups in a sensitive border area.[3]

Unfortunately the southern part of the Dobrudja was returned to Bulgaria in 1941, and the Vlachs were forced to move again. It is from this small area near Silistria that many emigrants in Germany and America originally came. One can understand their wish to preserve their Vlach identity. Deprived twice within thirty years of their homes, they are naturally bitter. It is said that many of the Vlachs of the southern Dobrudja played a prominent part in the Iron Guard or supported General Antonescu, but I have not been able to establish the truth of this report, although it would explain the strongly nationalistic and pro-Romanian sentiments of this particular sector of the Vlach diaspora.

The road to America and Germany was often a tortuous one. The Vlachs of the southern Dobrudja were moved to other areas of Yugoslavia. Some went to the Banat, where they joined a medley of other races, including Germans and Serbs.[4] After the Second World War Bessarabia was surrendered to the Russians, and the settlers in the Banat were joined by refugees from this area, another fragmented province consisting of Romanians, Ukrainians, Germans, Jews, Poles, Turks and Tartars.[5] But the break with Tito in 1948 meant that some of the Banat became too factious an area to be filled with ethnic fragments, and the poor Vlachs from the Dobrudja were forced to be on the move once more.

One of the places they moved to was a large labour camp near Slobozia, an undistinguished town in the Wallachian plain half way between Bucharest and the sea, slightly to the west of the Dobrudja proper. Slobozia has an unromantic name and appearance, large apartment blocks on the outside gradually giving way to dusty lanes full of sheep. The town has about fifty thousand inhabitants of whom about five thousand are Vlachs. Some of these were originally from the labour camp, while others had moved from the nearby Dobrudja. I visited the site of the labour camp in 1992, where four old inhabitants were still eking out a living. I spoke to them in my rudimentary Vlach and amazingly got a reply from one old lady who was an Ukrainian from Bessarabia settled in the Banat learning Vlach as a lingua franca.

Rather different were my experiences at the dinner dance of the Vlach association of Slobozia. This was a grand affair with six different courses and drinks served until five in the morning. In spite of the lavishness, proceedings were remarkably decorous, reminding me of dances in suburban Oxted during the late 1950s. Their dances were a little more intricate, but there was no drunken horseplay or amorous byplay, and I was able to carry on some historical research with the Chief of Police's daughter, a glamorous platinum blonde, benevolently nodding her approval by my side. I conducted most of my interviews with female students, speaking excellent English but also still speaking Vlach. They knew where their families had come from seventy years before, and clearly retained their identity. Vlach songs were sung, but there seemed no particularly strong political feeling. Nor did Vlachs originating from Voskopojë or Štip in Yugoslav

Macedonia or from Veroia in Greece seem to have any particular loyalty to their place of origin.

A year later I returned to Romania, intending to do some research in the northern Dobrudja among the Vlach villages there. Unfortunately I arrived in Bucharest in three feet of snow, and had to confine my researches to conversations with the academic community in Bucharest, Constanţa and Galaţi, observing the high hills of the Dobrudja across the Danube from the latter town. Romania has some distinguished historians and linguists of Vlach origin who have done most of the work recording the existence and continuity of Vlach villages in the Dobrudja.[6] Thus a visit from me would probably have been superfluous, although I would like to have done some work on where the Vlachs have come from and how far they have been able to preserve their identity. I was informed that the Vlachs from Veroia have been most easily assimilated, the Vlachs from Mount Grammos partly assimilated, but the Farsherots hardly assimilated at all.

The survival of the Vlachs as a separate group in Romania is remarkable for three reasons. In the first place we have the hardship and the moving from pillar to post, sadly familiar in Eastern Europe, but in the case of some of the Dobrudja Vlachs suffered by people who had only just been uprooted from their ancestral habitat. We can contrast the fate of refugees from Asia Minor after the Turkish-Greek war, most of whom have lost their special dialect and their identity, although occasionally the name of a village preserves, like Andromache's little Troy in the *Aeneid*, the memory of an ancient sorrow.[7] Secondly, unlike the Gaels, the Welsh and the Irish, where though belatedly special encouragement has been given to the language in educational and cultural spheres, Vlachs in Romania did not, as far as I know, receive even the limited help that was given to Vlachs in Greece between the wars.

Finally, the Vlachs in Romania appear to defy a fundamental law of linguistics. This law, elegantly stated by Professor Peter Trudgill, states that minority languages are most at risk when they fairly closely resemble the majority language of the state, and when they are a long way away from or in no way resemble the majority language of another state.[8] Thus Swedish in Finland is less vulnerable than Frisian in Germany because Swedish is very different from Finnish, being in an Abstand relationship with it, whereas Frisian is close to German, being in an Ausbau relationship with its fellow Teutonic tongue. Indeed the future of Frisian is gloomy, whereas Swedish in Finland is healthy. Elegantly and eloquently Trudgill shows that Greece by presenting Arvanitika and Vlachika as aberrant dialects of Greek rather than parts of the Albanian or Romanian language has helped to reduce the status of Albanian and Vlach in Greece.

My own observations of Vlach villages in Greece over the past twenty years correspond very closely to the findings of Trudgill and Tzavaros in the Albanian villages of Attica and Boiotia.[9] But it is possible to cast doubt on Trudgill's thesis, not only in the Balkans. We can begin at the other end of the Mediterranean. It is a little unwise to select Catalan as an example of a minority language in a weak position because it is in an Ausbau relationship with Spanish. Catalan ought to be particularly vulnerable because it is both an Ausbau language and also a true minority with no geographical contiguity with a major state language. Provençal or Occitan has probably helped Catalan, but it is a minority language threatened with extinction. On Trudgill's theory Catalan ought to be similarly threatened, but, as millions of Olympic games viewers know, it is Europe's most famous and healthy minority language, knocking on the door of the European community as an official language. If it achieves this status

Spanish might become vulnerable in Catalonia because of its Ausbau relationship with Catalan, while Provençal's position might improve because of its contiguity with a major language, although the French government is unlikely to be as accommodating as the Spanish. The decision to award Catalonia some kind of autonomy, the educational policy of the Catalonian authorities and the economic success of the Barcelona region are in stark contrast to the treatment of Albanian and Vlach by the Greek state, and have contributed to the rise of Catalan's fortunes, so different from the fate of the two Balkan minorities.

Trudgill tactfully plays down deliberate state interference, or more accurately lack of state support, as a factor in reducing Arvanitika and Vlachika to the status of a dialect, as opposed to that of Catalan, now nearly a state language. This reduction does support his thesis, but when we actually look at the Balkans as a whole there are some worrying arguments against it.

There are some other odd linguistic fragments in the Balkans which give rather a different picture. The Albanians of Greek Epirus, unlike those of Boiotia and Attica, speak a language virtually identical with the inhabitants of Albanian Epirus across the border. They cannot be passed off as a dialect of Greek, being in close contact with north Epirus until fifty years ago, and under the same administration eighty years ago. They ought to be in a stronger position than the Albanians of Attica and Boiotia, but though I have no first-hand research to back this up, apparently there is in the area west of Ioannina the same rapid decline of Albanian-speakers among the younger generation as we find further south.

Albanian ought to be stronger in Greek Epirus because it is geographically contiguous with a majority language and thus not a true minority language. It could be argued that the very real iron curtain between these two countries, briefly broken in 1992, and now it would seem tragically re-erected with the barriers on the other side to cope with the flood of refugees, did make the geographical contiguity an abstraction, but this defence would seem to be overruled when we cross the border into northern Epirus and start examining the Greeks and Vlachs of Albania. Here I have done some research and have to report that the position of Vlach and Greek in Albania is far healthier than the position of Vlach and Albanian in Greece, although on a theoretical level they should be exactly the same.[10]

Before the breakdown of Communism Greek survived fairly well in Albania. At times pressure was brought against communities, very often in connection with religion. Greek names of a religious nature were banned. Community leaders were imprisoned if they stepped out of line, but this was the case all over Albania. Attempts to preserve Greek culture were tolerated even if they were not exactly encouraged, except sporadically, perhaps in rare efforts to achieve a rapprochement with the Greek government. And Greek did survive in villages along the coast and in the Gjirokastër area.

Greek under the regime of Enver Hoxha, now a byword for infamy, was treated better than Albanian in Greece, the fountainhead of democracy, and therefore survived better. This simple fact cuts across all theory, although it could be argued that Greek, the language of Homer and Plato, has built-in advantages which ensures its survival in odd places like the Bronx and Tashkent and Calabria. Albanian too has survived in improbable quarters, including Italy, the United States and the Soviet Union, without authors as famous as Homer and Plato, and Vlach has survived without any authors at all. One of the places where Vlach has survived is Albania, although without any of the educational advantages of Greek. And so a theory can and must be modified by local historical circumstances. My last example confounding Ausbau and Abstand almost fatally results from my visit to Slobozia.

The survival of Vlach as distinct from Romanian in Romania seems to break all Trudgill's rules. In Slobozia I met several people whose family had originated from near Štip in eastern Macedonia. On the whole Vlachs even after two generations have preserved not only their language, but also their customs and identity. Calling themselves Macedo-Romanians or, even more confusingly and perhaps dangerously, Macedonians, they think of themselves as somehow distinct from the main body of Romanians. If we accept this view and regard Vlach as different from Romanian, it is an Ausbau language related to the majority language, not geographically contiguous with any other Vlachs. In this respect it is worse off than north Frisian, Trudgill's example of a very vulnerable language, but one which is at any rate fairly close to the Frisian of Holland.

The closest parallel I can think of to the Vlachs in Romania are the Pontic Greeks who arrived in Greece during the 1920s after the population exchanges between the Greeks and the Turks. My impression is that though Pontic Greeks have kept their dances and costumes, they have been less successful than the Vlachs of Romania in keeping their language, in spite of the fact that the time factor, the adverse circumstances under which the group arrived, and even the difference between the main language and the minority language is roughly the same in each case.

The survival of the Vlachs in Romania appears not only to break Trudgill's theoretical rules, but also to defy any of the practical economic or political explanations I have put forward for the survival of other minorities. It should perhaps be remembered that the Vlachs who arrived in Romania in the 1920s, some of whom subsequently emigrated to Germany and America, were very often Vlachs with a pro-Romanian stance. At Slobozia we began the dance with a kind of hymn to the Vlach language. It would be sentimental, unfashionable and almost certainly wrong to say that there is something in the Vlach character which helps the preservation of their language. Mussolini was rightly derided for his claims that the Italians were superior because of their descent from Roman legionaries. It could be argued that the harsh life of most Vlachs is a stern training for adversity, and the Slobozia Vlachs seem to have survived their troubles remarkably well. Perhaps the language has survived because of its character. It has never claimed to be the language of the intelligentsia, suitable for abstract thought, but is rather the language of the home, and it is in the Vlach homes that it has been preserved. Thus paradoxically Trudgill's reduction of Vlach from a language to a dialect may actually help its survival.

At this stage I say farewell to the Vlachs, although they emerge briefly in the next four chapters describing fragments at once more successful because more obtrusive and less successful because more truculent. The Pomaks like the Vlachs can be found in a number of different Balkan states, but are less well known, though more persecuted, more at risk, though less obviously distinctive. Other fragments in Greece, Macedonia and Kosovo are examined, where politics and journalism, controversy and danger are more apparent, in spite of widespread ignorance in the West about the past and present. It is possible that the Vlachs are a kind of model for other fragments and other Balkan troublespots.

6

The Pomaks

Pomakia sounds and is an invented Balkan country, too humble to be Ruritania and sounding suspiciously like the Slaka of Malcolm Bradbury's *Rates of Exchange*. But there is a fragment known as the Pomaks inhabiting the southern mountains of Bulgaria and the land across the border in north-eastern Greece. They are also to be found in scattered pockets in Yugoslav Macedonia, a fragment of fragments, and even in Albania.[1] Until now they have not hit the headlines in the same way as the schismatic Slovaks or beleaguered Bosnians, and it is to be hoped that they don't. It is perhaps in this hope that I write this account of my two weeks among the Bulgarian Pomaks rather in the manner of Bradbury's Dr Petworth, this frivolity being a mask for a concern for this people.

The Pomaks speak Bulgarian but are Muslims. This puts them in a peculiar position in all four countries I have named. In Bulgaria there is a large Turkish minority and a number of other minorities, notably the Pomaks and Gypsies, who are not Turkish but are Muslim.[2] At various times in the last forty years the Bulgarian government has moved against these Islamic groups, by for instance forcing them to change their Islamic names to Bulgarian, so that Ahmet became Asen. Many Turks fled to Turkey, but Pomaks without their linguistic advantages did not take this opportunity so often. In 1985 the Communist government in a last desperate attempt to gain popularity instituted a programme called the Process for Rebirth, in which mosques were destroyed. The Communist power was broken in 1989 and at the moment after a series of elections the party known as the Movement representing the Islamic minorities is in the happy position of holding the balance of power between the Socialist party, a thinly disguised version of the former Communists, and the Democratic party.[3]

This seems fortunate, and makes the Bulgarian Pomaks a great deal better off than their Greek equivalents. There are about 275,000 Bulgarian Pomaks and only about 25,000 Greek Pomaks. In Greece the official line has always been that there are no minorities, although there was some acceptance of a religious minority in western Thrace where the Pomaks live together with a larger number of ethnic Turks. There are also further to the west a number of Slav speakers who are orthodox in religion, and whom the Greeks briskly classify as Slav-speaking Greeks, not admitting the name Macedonian, although at any rate these Slavs do live in (Greek) Macedonia. I have not conducted any research among the Greek Pomaks, and it is difficult to do so since most Pomak villages are placed in a military zone, to penetrate which requires an official permit from Athens.[4] In Yugoslav Macedonia, as the Greeks do not allow us to say, the Pomaks as in Bulgaria find themselves competing with other Islamic minorities like Turks and Gypsies and in official statistics are liable to be disguised as Muslims, the official designation for Bosnians, with whose situation the problems of the Pomaks have several unfortunate if not exact parallels. In formerly Godless, but largely Muslim, Albania the few formerly Islamic Slav-speakers would seem to be now uniting with scattered pockets of Orthodox Slavs in the north and south of the country. There are probably about 25,000 Yugoslav and Albanian Pomaks.[5]

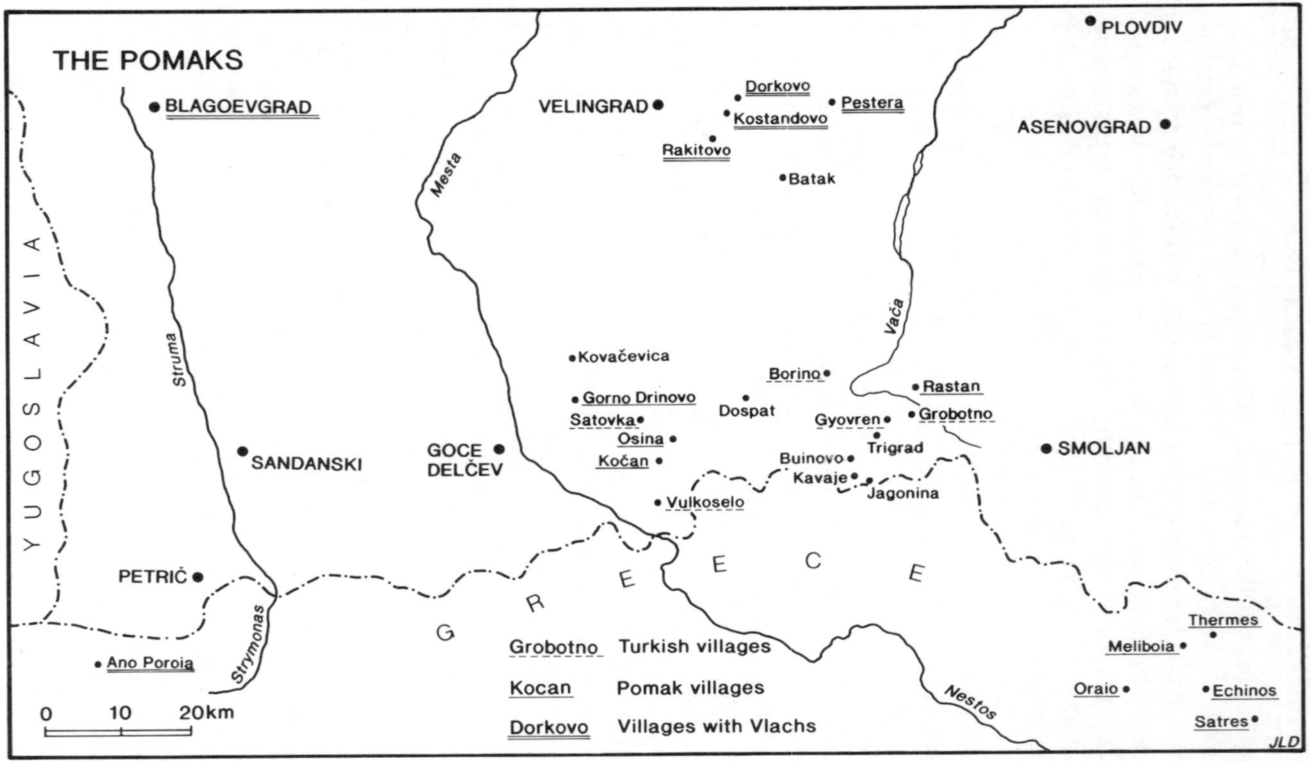

Map 6

THE POMAKS

YUGOSLAVIA

- BLAGOEVGRAD
- SANDANSKI
- VELINGRAD
- PLOVDIV
- ASENOVGRAD
- GOCE DELČEV
- PETRIČ
- SMOLJAN

Struma
Strymonas
Mesta
Vača
Nestos

- Ano Poroia
- Kovačevica
- Gorno Drinovo
- Satovka
- Osina
- Kočan
- Vulkoselo
- Dospat
- Borino
- Batak
- Rakitovo
- Kostandovo
- Dorkovo
- Pestera
- Rastan
- Grobotno
- Gyovren
- Trigrad
- Buinovo
- Kavaje
- Jagonina
- Meliboia
- Oraio
- Thermes
- Echinos
- Satres

GREECE

Grobotno   Turkish villages

Kočan   Pomak villages

Dorkovo   Villages with Vlachs

0   10   20km

JLD

Thus the Bulgarian Pomaks would find it difficult to form links with their fellow Pomaks. Even the name Pomak causes trouble. As is the case with Latin-speaking Vlachs, with whom the Pomaks are sometimes compared and confused, Pomak is a slightly derogatory term used by others to describe strangers whom they dislike. Both Vlach and Pomak are recognised by Vlachs and Pomaks as useful terms to describe themselves, but the useful terms are not welcomed. Most Vlachs now describe themselves as Aroumanians, but there is some doubt as to how the word should be spelt, and it does look suspiciously like Romanian. In Bulgaria the politically correct name for Pomaks is Bulgarian Muslims, something of a mouthful, and hardly useful for linking the Pomaks of Bulgaria with those of Greece.

I arrived in Sofia by train from Bucharest on August 4th 1992. The journey had about as much relation to the world of beautiful Balkan spies as I have to James Bond. In Sofia I joined an international team investigating the Pomaks, consisting of an American, an Englishman, a Turk, a Norwegian, a Czech and several Bulgarians. This sounds more impressive than it really was. Actually the team was very like that in Evelyn Waugh's *Scott King's Modern Europe.* On the other hand one cannot praise too highly the organiser of this team, Professor Julian Konstantinov of the University of Sofia, who coped with the difficulties of the next two weeks with Scott King's unflappability and James Bond's dynamism.

Professor Konstaninov works in the department of English Language at the University of Sofia. He became interested in the names of his students, and this led him to the problem of the minorities who had been forced to change their names. The science of onomastics, not a word to trip lightly off the tongue even in this pretentious pseudo-scientific age, is in fact an extremely useful device for establishing ethnic identity. It is not much use asking a giggling Pomak girl whether she considers herself a Bulgarian or a Pomak or a Turk, although we and Professor Konstantinov's team of research students did of course try this. It is useful to see how far, when offered free choice, the Pomaks had chosen to rename themselves, bearing in mind that they had three names to play with. They could go the whole hog and give themselves three Muslim names, and to do so would indicate some degree of radical Muslim fundamentalism. Many preferred to retain an -ov suffix in their final name. A village with a conservative policy of changing few names could usually be assumed to be one where the socialist party was powerful. We shall examine these oxymorons of radical/Muslim and conservative/socialist later in this chapter.

We began our study in the Bulgarian village of Kovačevica, a pictuesque village of crumbling old stone houses and an ageing entirely Bulgarian population. After two days of learned papers we went for a walk in the mountains and on our return met a delegation of village elders who maintained that it was disgraceful that we were meeting at all and, in rather a contradictory fashion, that it was disgraceful that our meeting was conducted in such a secretive fashion with the papers in English. It was as if the inhabitants of Leamington Spa objected to the University of Warwick discussing as it frequently does in a conference organised by the Institute of Ethnic Relations problems of ethnicity in the West Midlands. In making this comparison I have deliberately increased the size of the units, since Kovačevica is far smaller than Leamington Spa and our conference was a very small affair. Nevertheless the dispute reached the national newspapers in Bulgaria.

The good burghers of Kovačevica felt that we were upsetting the Pomaks, but our reception in the next ten days argued against this. Next day we went to the nearby village of Gorno Drinovo, an entirely Pomak village with a Democratic mayor who was extremely helpful. We looked at the name changes, where most had retained the -ov suffix, and asked some women in a clothing factory, sewing bags for an Austrian firm, whether they thought of themselves as Pomaks or Turks or Bulgarian Muslims. Only one called herself a Turk. She was wearing the typical Muslim baggy trousers. The mayor gave us lots of beer, but we stayed the night with a leader of the fundamentalist party who offered us nothing stronger than very strong black coffee. Trousers, names and drinks are a good, quick, but not infallible guide to political opinions and ethnic identity; we were later to discover the equivalent of Labour voters taking the *Daily Telegraph* for the sake of the crossword.

Our fundamentalist host told us tales of persecution, beginning with his grandfather who had been flayed alive oh a cherry tree when Bulgaria had taken control of the village in 1912. In Kovačevica there were notices in the church Bible of the whole village fleeing to the hills in the Balkan War of 1912 and the earlier unsuccessful Ilinden rising of 1903. As in Yugoslavia where people are repaying old scores of the 1940s, so in Bulgaria memories of cruelty and repression last a long time. And in spite of Mr Gladstone there was cruelty and repression on both sides. In a melancholy and slightly mad way our host apologised for being so rude about Christians as he explained his own personal persecutions. He had changed his name to a fully Muslim one and wanted to take his family to Turkey, although he spoke no Turkish. We visited the Mosque where there was a new Koran presented by the Government of Iran with a picture of the Ayatollah Khomeini in it. I felt a sneaking return of sympathy for the citizens of Kovačevica.

We returned to Kovačevica and next day visited the small town of Satovka. Here Pomaks, Bulgarians and Gypsies lived harmoniously together. Bulgarians had apparently defended the Pomaks in the bad times. We conducted questionnaires among both Pomaks and Bulgarians over a lot of drinks and considerable hilarity. No doubt a similar superficial judgement of racial integration has been made about several towns in Bosnia now sullied by ethnic cleansing. There was no hotel in Satovka and we had to go about ten miles up the road to an extraordinary place of superficial luxury and grandeur but with no food. It really only functioned as a rather dubious night club with gypsy girls taking their clothes off, although I did not pursue my enquiries into this particular ethnic phenomenon.

Next day we made a brief visit to Osina, apparently a Pomak village with a majority voting for the Socialists, but the mayor could not find the key to this office and so we were unable to get access. We then went to Kočan, a village with a democratic majority but a socialist mayor of an old family whose grandfather had also been mayor. The mayor was very gloomy about unemployment. In these villages the men sat around while the women worked at their tobacco crop. There was seasonal employment picking mushrooms, but many factories had been closed. Battered Ladas and large houses proclaimed better days. We visited some Gypsies who seemed prosperous in the new capitalist Bulgaria. I felt ill and visited a doctor who, though overworked, came in, took my blood pressure and kindly said I was suffering from a sore throat.

So I slept through another night of the gypsy girls, who made a terrible noise, and next day visited the radical village of Vulkoselo, or Wolf's Town, where there was a majority for the Movement. The old men spoke Turkish.

They were building a new mosque, the old one having been pulled down in 1987 by the Process of Rebirth party who had built instead a Palace of Culture with a new library. I felt a rather odd tug of loyalties between the new and the old in this odd village where some of the little girls wore baggy trousers and we had a meal of pork and beer.

The mayor, aged twenty-eight, was an intelligent young man, eager to find employment for his fellow citizens. We were shown a factory originally making overalls, where many machines lay idle, as did the men of the village while their womenfolk worked on the tobacco crop. Assuming mistakenly that I and my American colleague were men of power and influence in the world of commerce he asked us about foreign investment. We discouraged the tobacco trade as a long-term answer and instead encouraged him to look at cottage trades like weaving, of which we saw some fine specimens. We even met a middleman in the shape of an American citizen who had escaped first to Greece in 1972 and then to New Jersey, returning recently. The mayor was also hopeful that the Greek frontier might be reopened nearby, and that access to the White Sea, as he rather charmingly called the Mediterranean, would improve prospects of trade. We could see Greece from the village and wished him well, although Bulgaria's recognition of independent Macedonia has not helped matters.

The mayor seemed interested in history. He said there were some Roman remains four miles down the valley, although later he said these belonged to a Crusader castle. He said that old tombstones proved that the village had been lived in since the thirteenth century, although sadly when we looked at these tombstones they proved to be dated in years of the Muslim era and belonged to the early nineteenth century. He said that when the mosque had been destroyed an old stone had been found and then lost, as had a camel's head, and that these really did prove that the Pomaks had come to the village in pre-Ottoman times.[6]

The Bulgarians like to think that the Pomaks are Bulgarians forcibly converted to Islam. There is evidence of this happening in certain cases. As with the Bosnians the conversion may have been voluntary and late, although the two cases are not exactly the same, since the Bosnians were not conquered until much later and they lay in an uneasy borderline between Catholic and Orthodox spheres of influence with the Bogomil heresy adduced by some scholars as an additional contributory factor. None of these explanations work for the Pomaks. The Turks like to think of the Pomaks as Turks who have been forced to speak Bulgarian, and there is of course evidence in very recent times of Pomaks being forcibly encouraged to think of themselves as Bulgarians in just this way. But the Pomaks are not Turks, as we saw when we went to a real Turkish village in Bulgaria. Among other things there is a high proportion of Pomaks who have fair hair. This rather encourages the more romantic theories of Greek historians who are anxious to prove that the Pomaks are really Greek. They talk wistfully of an ancient tribe, the Athinganoi in this area at the time of Alexander the Great or even earlier, but are also prepared to accept the pre-Ottoman Turk theory as this would prove that the Pomaks as part of the Byzantine Empire, were really Greeks. There were undoubtedly Turkish-speaking tribes like the Cumans and the Pechenegs who invaded across the Danube in the eleventh century, and Turkish-speaking mercenaries were brought in before the Ottomans in the fourteenth century.[7]

It is probably futile to speculate on the origin of the Pomaks. A real romantic would investigate the Crusader castle and decide that the Pomaks were the descendants of the army of the Latin Emperor of Constantinople, Baldwin of Flanders, who disappeared in somewhat mysterious circumstances campaigning against the Bulgarians.[8] I have heard more absurd explanations of the origin of the Vlachs. In a vague way anxious to see if there was any evidence for a crusader presence I took a bus to the town of Goce Delčev where there was a museum, but this was unfortunately closed.

Goce Delčev was a hero of the struggle against the Turks and is very popular in Yugoslavian Macedonia where there are streets named after him. He is even popular among the Pomaks because he had a Turkish mother and appears to have been a genuine Robin Hood, fighting everywhere for the oppressed irrespective of racial or religious considerations, unlike Sandanski, the name of another Bulgarian town and the name of another freedom-fighter supposed to be responsible for the death of twenty-three thousand Muslims. Goce Delčev was a good Bulgarian name for the Communist government to use to replace the original Greek name of Nevrokop. For until 1912 Nevrokop was one of the most northerly bastions of Hellenism with a ferociously pro-Greek bishop whose fulminations in classical Greek against Bulgars and Vlachs I have read with some pleasure.[9]

The hotel in Goce Delčev is known as the Nevrokop. It is pretentious, noisy and uncomfortable, but cheap and friendly. I rang up my wife from the neighbouring post office as easily and cheaply as I would ring up from Guildford. There are churches and streets which look very Greek, although these streets with names like Bitola, Serres and even Solun (Salonica) seem to point to Nevrokop's greater Bulgarian aspirations. The first woman I spoke to knew some Greek, but I heard no Greek in the colourful market where the Gypsies and Bulgarians seemed to be selling pairs of pants and semi-pornographic videos more successfully than the Pomaks were selling their peppers.

We hitched a lift with a friendly Pomak from the eastern part of the country who said he was visiting his wife in Goce Delčev. It seemed an improbable tale, but fortunate for us, as the bus station on market day looked confusing. The Pomak's car had a defective battery and was short on petrol, but somehow in spite of getting lost we reached Dospat where the heroic Professor Konstantinov had coped with the loss of our original driver. He had gone off in a huff, having had too many Pomaks or not enough gypsy girls, but the manager of the gypsy girls had found us a less comfortable van but a much more enterprising driver.

So it was off on Saturday to Borino, a Turkish village where children only started learning Bulgarian at school. There seemed more confidence and cleanliness here. No trousers, but a flourishing mosque, no alcohol at lunch, but far too much at dinner in a cheese factory where they had slaughtered a turkey in our honour. The Turks in Bulgaria are found in two main pockets in the south east and north east of the country; Borino is an extension of the south east pocket. Confusion with Pomaks is extensive, but of course the Turks don't like the association, and no Turk wants to be called a Pomak, although several Pomaks want to be called Turks. Indeed one of the troubles about the term Pomak is that for the pro-Turkish party among the Pomaks it sounds too Bulgarian, while for the pro-Bulgarian party it sounds too Turkish.

We found some of the latter when we set off for the border up some rugged gorges for three strongly socialist villages, Buinovo, Kavaje and Jagonina. The river Vača fights its way through the limestone, sometimes going underground to form huge caves, before descending to the southern Bulgarian plain at Plovdiv, where it is called the

Maritza, and then oddly wending its way back southwards to form as the Evros the Greek-Turkish border. A strange journey, although not as strange as that taken by defectors from East Germany who, rather than trying to escape across the Wall, used to take holidays on the Bulgarian Black Sea coast, work their way inland and then try to cross this difficult border. The terrain is rugged, and the border which we saw was formidable. Two and a half kilometres from the actual frontier there is an enormous fence, electrically controlled and covered with barbed wire. Nobody lives inside the fencing, although there are some barracks. Only a few people even today are allowed inside the fence. Outside the fence there are two border zones, and those in the zone nearest to the fence were compulsorily moved after the war, though then allowed to return. Not surprisingly, not many escaped across this border.

More surprising is the loyalty of these villages to the old socialist order. Deprived of much of their land in the forbidden zone, the villages seemed poor and run down. The land is too high in these parts to grow tobacco. A factory making spare parts for armaments had been closed down. Were the border with Greece to be opened, there might be a tourist attraction in the shape of vast caves, one full of impressive stalactites, the other a horrible mixture of Dante's *Inferno* and Alton Towers, with dimly lit caverns and high staircases supported shakily by slimy rotting iron handrails. Some capitalist investment would be necessary here.

The strongly socialist villages were hostile to the idea of being thought anything but Bulgarian. Mosques had been destroyed or neglected, Muslim names had been rarely taken except by a few old people. Nevertheless our reception was warm. There was no restaurant in Buinovo, but a complete stranger supplied us with an excellent lunch.

It was thought that he was frightened that we belonged to some international commission come to inspect the workings of the collective farm. In Buinovo in 1912 the villagers had fled to Greece, and in 1948 they had been moved to the northern part of the country, but had shown surprising loyalty to their place of origin.

The next day we went to another socialist village, Trigrad, two Turkish villages, Gyovren and Grobotno, and one Pomak village, Rastan, where we bargained in a sordid fashion for rugs. Trigrad was like the other socialist villages, Rastan the usual mixture, but the two Turkish villages were remarkable for history and drunkenness. In one of them modestly drinking a bottle of beer I found myself locked into the inn, forced to watch an American film with Greek subtitles dubbed into Bulgarian, because no fewer than three men had had to be escorted unsteadily out and then refused admission. In the next village I found two men round a table inspecting a bagpipe, another slumped in a stupor, another wildly dancing. The dancer invited me to join him and this roused his drunken companion and we shuffled round the floor. Who can tell the dancer from the dance? I could.

I am unable to explain this degree of inebriation. Professor Konstantinov, working while I was drinking and dancing, had discovered the name Yuruk as a surname frequent in Grobotno. The Yuruks were a nomadic tribe from Asia whom the Turks had settled at various stages in their conquest of the Balkan peninsula, usually in mountainous areas because of their abilities as transhumant pastoralists. They had retained something of their identity as somehow different from the Turks.[10] An Asiatic cast of features was noticeable in some cases. I don't know if drunkenness is a peculiarly Yuruk feature. The village had two mosques, one a new one in the plain below, built to replace a mosque on the same site, the latter apparently going back to the fifteenth century when it had been built in honour of Ibrahim Pasha.

The next day we left the Pomaks, travelling northwards through the Rhodopes through Batak to Peštera. Batak is a grim place, but one important for Bulgarian and even English history. In 1876 the Bulgarians rose against the Turks and drove them southwards, but the Turks came back and slaughtered the Bulgarians. We saw the skulls preserved in grisly fashion in the church, where 2,000 had been killed. The word used to describe the slaughterers was 'bashibazouks', a word used by Gladstone in his Midlothian address when he rose up in fury after retiring from politics to denounce the supine attitude of the British government to the Bulgarian atrocities. From Batak we can trace the fall of Disraeli, the triumphant return of Gladstone and even the abortive treaty of San Stefano which awarded almost the whole of the southern Balkans to Bulgaria in 1878, although this was rescinded, and the Pomaks remained under Ottoman rule for another thirty-four years.

This was perhaps fortunate because the bashibazouks whom Gladstone wanted to send bag-and-baggage across the Bosphorus were partly, if not mostly Pomaks, irregular local troops fighting on behalf of the Turks. And so the Pomaks enter English history, and it is time to drop the pen of Dr Petworth and take up the sword of Rudolf Rassendyl in order to try and do something for these poor people, battered by history, torn in so many different directions, unable to find an identity, divided and unemployed, their past full of violence, their present full of poverty, their future full of uncertainty.

Of course these problems are not unique in the Balkans or even in Bulgaria. Bosnia has raised Europe's awareness of the problem of the Balkan fragments. The Bosnian Muslims are in many ways like the Pomaks, a religious minority speaking the majority language in a country full of linguistic and religious minorities. Bulgaria's transition from Communism to democracy has been achieved without violence, as in Romania, or anarchy, as in Albania, or terrible ethnic strife, as in Yugoslavia. I wrote my account of the Pomaks in Peštera, a charming sleepy town on the foothills of the Rhodope mountains. There are no Pomaks but a host of Gypsies and, as in 1982, I met some Vlachs and Karakatchans, Greek-speaking pastoralists. A factory seemed to be closed, leaving a horrible smell, but there did not appear to be any great unhappiness or poverty either in the large gypsy mahala or in the pretentious Soviet-style main street and square with its lavish public buildings or the old-fashioned nineteenth-century streets leading off it. There are two enormous hotels, but only one seemed to be working, and we found with difficulty a squalid restaurant, full of pictures of heroic workers and drunken priests, presumably a relic of Communist propaganda. But different races and time periods seem to be working together in Peštera, so why not in Pomakia.

The answer I fear lies in history and religion. Religious minorities have had an even less happy history than the Vlachs and Gypsies of Peštera. The Vlachs and Gypsies like the Welsh and Gaels have been persecuted. They have not met evil with evil. This is not the case in what was Yugoslavia and still is Northern Ireland and what may be Pomakia.

Then there is the economic factor. It is hard to think of ways to improve the economic position of the Pomaks. Tourism seems a possibility. They have the empty hotels and the caves with the rotting handrails, the weaving and the gypsy girls, the mountains and the lakes, a friendly people, some impressive buildings. What they lack is the infrastructure. All over Eastern Europe people are trying to become capitalists without any capital. When this does not work they tend to turn on each other. Countries which have greeted the overthrow of Communism as a triumph of the human spirit and the free-market economy should feel guilty when the collapse of the free-market economy twists the human spirit in ugly directions.

Greek Fragments

'Den echome meionotētes.' We do not have minorities. Such is the defiant cry of many a Greek politician and historian. But there are fragments of Greek speech outside Greece and fragments of non-Greek speech inside Greece, and in this minority-conscious age these fragments are beginning to assume an importance disproportionate to their actual numbers. In the past these numbers were much larger.

In 1912, still within living memory, the northern frontiers of Greece roughly coincided with those we associate with Classical Greece. Thessaly and Aetolia were Greek, but Macedonia and Epirus, semi-Greek in Classical times, were still under Turkish rule, although many Greek-speakers lived there as did some speakers of languages other than Greek who through religious, commercial or educational ties felt themselves Greeks. Both kinds of Greeks also lived along the shores of the northern and eastern Aegean and along the coastline of the Black Sea, as they had done since Classical times.

By being on the winning side in both Balkan wars and the First World War, Greece gained far more territory. In 1913 she was rewarded with Epirus and Macedonia, and after the Great War, in which Turkey and Bulgaria were on the wrong side, she was given western Thrace which had briefly become Bulgarian. For a short time Greece also had possession of eastern Thrace which we now know as Turkey in Europe, and a sizeable portion of Asia Minor near Smyrna. There then followed the disastrous war against the resurgent Turkey of Kemal Ataturk, at the end of which under the Treaty of Lausanne in 1923 the Turks regained what they had lost. Subsequently there was a massive exchange of populations. Over a million Greeks left Asia Minor to be settled in Europe, while a much smaller number of Turks left Greece for Turkey. Similar exchanges on a less dramatic scale took place between Greece and Bulgaria.[1]

As a result of these exchanges Greece had to give up the rather quaintly entitled Great Idea, the aim of recovering her Byzantine power on both sides of the Aegean. But she gained a much more compact and ethnically homogeneous state. The immigrants assimilated easily, and, though names of Macedonian villages like Nea Smyrna, Nea Marmara and Neos Kaukasos may suggest nostalgia for the past, the new arrivals were quick and eager to take part in the life of modern Greece. They were a great improvement on the large and potentially disloyal Turkish population they replaced. The exchange of populations might almost seem like an advertisement for what we now have come to know as ethnic cleansing, although in contrast to modern ethnic cleansing this exchange was carried out with the full cooperation of both governments. In addition material progress over the past seventy years has meant that victims of population exchanges now have more to lose when they are transferred from one country to another.[2]

In 1913 Greeks had actually been in a minority in Macedonia and western Thrace; by 1928 the number of Greek-speakers had doubled as a result of the influx of refugees.[3] After the population exchanges there were very few Greek speakers living outside Greek territory, unless we count those who had emigrated to America or Australia, and in Greece there were comparatively few whose first language was not Greek. Time has done much to diminish

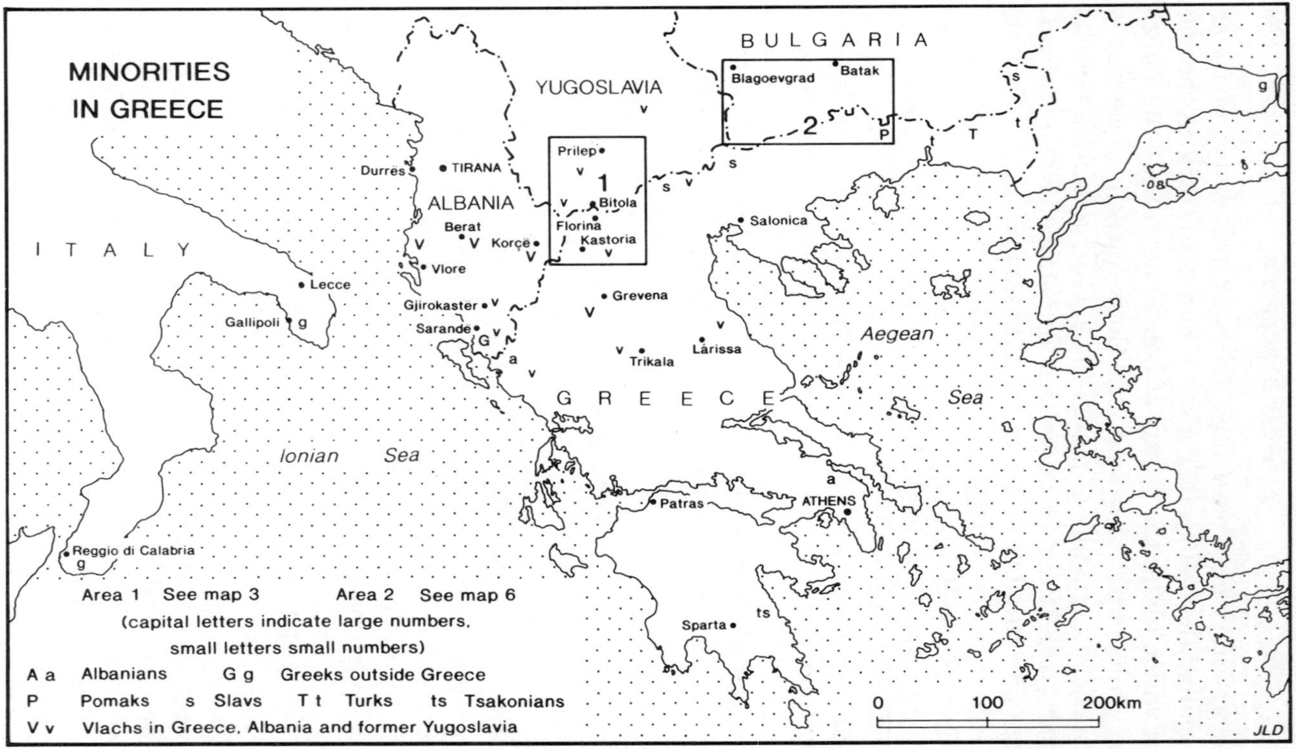
MINORITIES
IN GREECE
BULGARIA
YUGOSLAVIA
ALBANIA
ITALY
GREECE
Blagoevgrad
Batak
Prilep
Bitola
Florina
Kastoria
Durrës
TIRANA
Berat
Korçë
Vlore
Lecce
Gallipoli
Gjirokastër
Sarandë
Grevena
Trikala
Lárissa
Salonica
Patras
ATHENS
Sparta
Reggio di Calabria
Ionian Sea
Aegean Sea
Area 1 See map 3
Area 2 See map 6
(capital letters indicate large numbers,
small letters small numbers)
A a Albanians
G g Greeks outside Greece
P Pomaks
s Slavs
T t Turks
ts Tsakonians
V v Vlachs in Greece, Albania and former Yugoslavia
0
100
200km
JLD

Map 7

the size of both kinds of fragment, and with a little more time and a little luck they might have vanished completely. Unfortunately events in the past five years have suddenly inflated the importnace of minorities all over the Balkans, and the Greeks cannot escape the consequences of the problems caused by these fragments, who obstinately refuse to go away.

Of the indigenous Greeks living outside Greece there is only one group likely to cause political difficulty. In Albania there are Greek-speakers along the coast north and south of Sarande and in the Drin valley near Gjirokastër. In both world wars Greece briefly occupied this area and the territory around Korçë which it once claimed as a Greek city, although the claims would seem to be based on the strength of the Greek Orthodox religion and the presence of a certain number of Vlachs. But along the coast in villages like Himarë and in the Drin valley the children still speak Greek, and in the 1991 election the Greeks put up their own candidates for a party called Omonoia and won two seats. In the elections of 1992 for some reason this was not allowed, although there was a party claiming to stand for ethnic rights.

Greece only recently abandoned its claim to the territory it knew as northern Epirus. There is still an active lobby for northern Epirus, working abroad. In 1983 in an airport hotel in Chicago I stumbled into the dinner dance of the local Northern Epirote association, and found myself in a distinctly underdressed minority. Periodically this lobby and Greeks within Greece claim that there is discrimination against Greek-speakers. But the Hoxha regime did allow some educational rights, and Greek newspapers faithfully reporting the party line were printed.

At the moment the position is complicated. Greek-speaking Albanians are in the forefront of those seeking to leave their country in search of employment. This must make any statistics for Greek-speakers hard to calculate. Greek gifts, material and spiritual, may influence some of the population. Churches in Greek-speaking villages attracted priests from Greece. In 1993 a pro-Greek bishop was expelled. In the same year we saw notices demanding Greek schools both in the Drin valley and along the coast. Clearly not all villages have educational rights. There is considerable bilingualism and even trilingualism, making numbers even more incalculable.[4]

The history of the Greek villages is also hard to write. There is some evidence that the settlements along the coast are ancient ones. Greeks have always hugged the coast since Classical times, and the Byzantine Empire had more control of the Adriatic coast than the interior. Resistance against the Turks by the inhabitants of Himarë has been claimed as part of Albania's fight for freedom, but the leaders of this revolt probably spoke Greek. In contrast the Greeks of the Drin valley are probably more recent arrivals. Travelling in these parts at the beginning of the nineteenth century the English physician Henry Holland found only 140 families out of 4,000 who spoke Greek in Gjirokastër, or Argyro Kastro as it was known then, and placed the Greek/Albanian linguistic frontier at Delvinaki well to the south.[5] Events in both world wars involved considerable forced movements of population with Greek villages particularly vulnerable.[6]

Other Greek-speaking enclaves outside Greece are of more interest to philologists than to politicians. There are two tiny fragments of Greek-speakers in Apulia and Calabria. Their Greek, heavily interlarded now with Italian, is an archaic dialect which would appear to go back to Classical times, although reinforced in the Byzantine and Turkish epoch. It seems rather sad that this dialect will die out, but it is now spoken only by the old. Efforts from Greece, encouraged by the Italian government, to keep the dialect going by, for instance, encouraging exchange visits of schoolchildren, are of little help, since the archaic dialect under such conditions will lose out to standard Greek.[7]

In Turkey, because the population exchanges were conducted on religious rather than linguistic lines, there are still a few Greek-speaking Muslims whose language is again interesting because of its archaic features and its corruption by Turkish.[8] In the former Soviet Union there were communities speaking an odd kind of Greek in Odessa, the Crimea and at Mariupol and Rostov on the Sea of Azov.[9] Stalin moved most of these to Tashkent where they were joined by pro-Communist refugees from the Civil War. There are moves to repatriate this group to Greece. Finally in Bulgaria there are a few Greek-speakers near Burgas, the remnants of a much larger population along the coast who were exchanged with Bulgarian-speakers in Greece.[10] There are also the Sarakatsans, known as the Karakatchans in Bulgaria. These are Greek-speaking transhumants often confused with the Vlachs, with whom they profess to be at enmity. Under the Communists the Karakatchans survived and flourished, being in demand for their skill in managing sheep and goats in collective farms on the high pastures. I met some in 1982 and noticed their straight noses, although I was unable to detect any archaic features in their dialect. Some fancifully like to think of them as ancient Greeks who somehow missed out on the Dorian invasion and the whole Classical and Byzantine period which followed. Sarakatsans in Greece have largely abandoned their traditional way of life, and have either settled or moved as gastarbeiter to Germany. The Greek government apparently welcomes applications by Karakatchans to move to Greece.[11]

In Greece itself there are a number of non-Greek and semi-Greek fragments who have continued to hold out, although in many cases their existence is precarious. The

Ladin community of Spanish-speaking Jews in Salonica would appear to have perished in the Second World War. The Nazi regime was equally unkind to Gypsies, but these have survived, although not in such numbers as in the former Yugoslavia, Bulgaria and Romania, where some are suffering and some flourishing in the chaotic post-Communist era. Gypsies are notoriously adept at picking up the language of the area in which they are living, while preserving their own private argot. The whole subject of gypsy dialects in the Balkans is so complex that it seems hardly surprising that the best work on them was done by a British diplomat in the First World War. Special vocabularies used by certain communities as a private language can also be found in Greece.[12]

In the eastern Peloponnese there is a dialect, Tsakonian, spoken by a few old people in five villages. This dialect is supposed to derive from ancient Spartan, and as in the case of the Greek of southern Italy it seems sad that such a link with the past should be broken.[13] In northern Greece where emigrés from Anatolia settled after the exchange of populations, some retain a distinct dialect, almost unintelligible to the average Greek. This is particularly true of the Pontic Greeks coming from towns like Trabzon on the Black Sea. I have twice heard men of my generation hearing my bad modern Greek interspersed with Classical Greek say politely that I spoke in the same way that their fathers spoke. This anecdotal evidence would suggest that most Pontic Greeks abandon their archaic dialect and learn to speak standard Greek within a generation. Because of the religious criterion for the population exchange it is also possible to find intermingled with Asiatic Greek-speakers inhabitants who speak Turkish or even the languages of the Caucasus. Armenians came over both as traders before 1912 and as refugees after 1923, and form a sizeable minority in their own right.[14] Laz, a Georgian language, hardly recognised in the Soviet Union, can be found in Greece.[15]

None of these minorities present any particular political problem. They are interesting for philologists and historians, and their eventual extinction would be regrettable. The latter statement would be true for four more sensitive political minorities, the Vlachs, the Albanians, the Slavs and the Turks. The Vlachs, dealt with at length in earlier chapters of this book, are the easiest minority for the Greeks to handle. All but a very few old women speak Greek as well as Vlach. In all but a few villages Vlach is no longer spoken by the children. The language is not encouraged in any way, and even the Vlachs themselves seem to think it a bit of a joke. By downgrading it to a dialect, and a dialect with a slightly derogatory name the Greeks have helped the demise of the language.[16] Historians stress the links between the Vlachs and the Greeks. Many Vlachs have achieved prominence as Greek statesmen.[17] Between the wars there were schools financed by the Romanian government and, in the Second World War, a not very successful attempt by the Italians to foster pro-Latin sentiment among the Vlachs. These were counter-productive. Those with pro-Romanian or pro-Vlach feelings tended to emigrate. It is among these emigrés from Greece and other Balkan countries where the Vlachs are less likely to speak Greek, although many of them still do, that agitation for Vlach rights is conspicuous. This agitation has hardly been successful; perhaps its only result has been that research among the Vlachs in Greece might now be more difficult to conduct. No difficulties have been put in my way.

Albanian speakers are found in some villages of Attica and Boiotia, the remains of a much larger population in southern Greece, including the islands of Salamis and Hydra, and also in north-western Greece near the Albanian border. In both areas the language is in decline, with few young people speaking it. The Albanians near the border, known as the Tsams, were suspected of collaboration with the Axis during the war and suffered during and after it. No allowance is made in either area for the existence of the language, which has a humble status. The Albanians of the south have not been in contact with Albania proper for a long time, and they speak a language very different from standard Albanian. This is less true of Albanians in Epirus, but by some quirk of linguistic geography these are not to be found on the actual border but a little further south, and in any case because of politics there has been no cross-border contact for forty-five years. There is little communication between the two groups in Greece. The lack of contact with Albania has encouraged the view that Arvanitika (Greek Albanian), a name distinct from Alvanika (Albanian proper), is, like Vlach, an almost comic dialect rather than a proper language.[18]

At the beginning of this century the dividing line between Greek- and Slav-speakers lay well to the south of the present border, although there were isolated pockets of Greek speakers in towns north of the border like Bitola, Strumica, Petrič and Nevrokop (now Goče Delčev).[19] Population exchanges and generations of educational neglect have greatly reduced the number of Slav-speakers, but it is possible to find them well to the south of Florina. The Greeks briskly refer to Slav-speaking Greeks, and there may be something in this title, since originally the division between those loyal to Greece and those not was religious rather than linguistic, depending on whether the inhabitants supported the Patriarchist Greek church or Exarchist Bulgarian church. Moreover the Slav-speakers if they are not Greek are in certain difficulties about exactly what nation they do belong to. Florina is a long way from Bulgaria, and the language spoken near Florina is a long way from Serbian, the official language north of the border before 1939 and oddly not particularly close to standard Macedonian, the rather artificial language created after 1945.

Until recently communications between Bitola and Florina were quite easy, with a good motor road and even a comically slow train for travellers anxious to take advantage of shopping bargains. This probably helped the language, as did the return to Greece under various amnesties of pro-Communist sympathisers who had been refugees in Yugoslavia and other Slav-speaking countries. A large proportion of the workforce used to work as gastarbeiter in Germany, where they would meet Slavs as well as Greeks, before returning with temporary wealth to their village. The village of Grivas near Salonica seemed full of Slav-speakers who had returned home to set up restaurants serving beer and wienerschnitzel.

Further south, adjoining the southern part of Bulgaria there is another problem. The Slav-speakers here live in a military area and are difficult to visit, as until recently were people in the area north of the border, west of Goce Delčev. This is the land of the Pomaks, but the Greek Pomaks are sadly in an almost worse plight than their Bulgarian cousins. Contact across the closely guarded border was impossible until a few years ago, but is still very difficult. Oddly, the Greek Pomaks are not exactly contiguous with the Bulgarian Pomaks to the north west. The road north of Ehinos, the largest Greek Pomak centre, does not actually lead anywhere, but if it did it would come out not among the Bulgarian Pomaks west of Smoljan, but among the Bulgarian Turks to the east. To the south the road from Ehinos leads to Xanthi, where there are plenty of Turks, but Xanthi is a long way away from the Slav-speakers near Salonica, with whom the Pomaks have little contact and little in common. Both in official policy and in official statistics the Greek Pomaks fall somewhat uneasily between the hardly steady stools of the Greek Slavs and the Greek Turks.[20]

The latter minority is the largest in Greece, and the only one that the Greek government recognises, although in the rather peculiar form of counting them as a religious rather than a linguistic minority. As such they have special schools, although by going to these schools the Turks hardly qualify themselves for taking a major part in Greek educational, social or commercial life. There used to be members of parliament representing this minority, but these have run into certain difficulties recently. Figures in Greek accounts for this particular fragment are almost certainly an underestimate. Such figures would include some Pomaks, but not Christian Turks who did not join the post-Lausanne population exchange or Turkish-speaking Christians who came over in this exodus. Eccentrically, the Treaty of Lausanne allowed Muslims in western Thrace to stay put. A similar clause allowed Greeks to remain in Istanbul, but all but a handful of such Greeks have now left.[21] Until recently the Turks of western Thrace did not seem to matter very much. In bilingual towns like Komotini relations between Greeks and Turks seem fairly peaceful. But it is odd to see no bilingual notices in this town, and there is something strange about names like 'Mustapha' in Greek capital letters.[22]

This analysis of their fragments does not show the Greeks in a very good light. Recent sensitivity about the possibility of the Yugoslav province of Macedonia becoming an independent state spring partly from a feeling that Greece's claim to Greek Macedonia is made weaker by the existence of non-Greek fragments in this area. In addition to the furious insistence that the name 'Macedonia' belongs to Greece, those on the Greek side are contemptuous of the claim of the Yugoslav Macedonians to be a nation, stressing the heterogeneous population of what they like to call 'the republic of Skopje'. Such contempt suggests that everyone in Greece is totally Greek, and this is the official line.

It is possible to have some sympathy for this line. Greeks are naturally proud of their language, the language of Homer and the New Testament, of Aeschylus and Plato, and a contemptuous attitude to Vlach, Albanian, Slav and Turkish is understandable if not desirable. Of course the average Greek villager is not Homer or Plato; on the contrary, there are problems of illiteracy in Greece, and we can understand how governments might think that these problems would be compounded if other languages were taught in schools. English people moving to Wales face similar agitations if they have children of school age.

Then there is the current and pressing problem of refugees. Albania, Bulgaria and the fragmented Yugoslavia do not have very stable regimes, and their citizens face considerable economic problems. Turkey is relatively steady, but refugees from the Caucasus and Kurds have worked their way to Turkey's western frontier in order to gain access to the safe haven of the European Community. Greece's long tradition of hospitality to strangers has been taxed for many years by hordes of tourists, but at least tourists go away and are usually quite rich. This is not the case with refugees from former Communist countries, whose claims to enter, and ease of entry, are much improved if they have members of their race living within the borders of Greece.

And then there is the example of the former Yugoslavia. Here was a nation that appeared to thrive by encouraging minorities, that used to boast of its fragmented parts as making up a unified whole. Yugoslav Macedonia, itself the embodiment of a slightly dubious minority, barely recognised until 1945, allowed educational rights to Turks and

Albanians. In the past three years there has even been talk of allowing the Vlachs of Macedonia similar privileges. And yet Yugoslavia is now being torn apart, and the careful recording of ethnic statistics has now been replaced by the hideous process of ethnic cleansing. The Albanian minority in Macedonia is causing difficulty, as indeed is the Turkish minority in Bulgaria and the Greek minority in Albania. How much better, it could be argued, to deny the existence of languages other than Greek in Greece and to publish no statistics of ethnic minorities. Prizren in Kosovo has street signs in three languages, Albanian, Turkish and Serbian, while Metsovo, the largest Vlach centre in the Balkans, has nothing written except in Greek. Which is the happier place?

And yet the Greek policy has not quite worked and is not quite right. Minorities are now in the news. There are powerful and vocal groups working for them in Western Europe, perhaps most notably the Catalans, an example of a fragment which has emerged as a cohesive force after years of oppression. This oppression has tended to make the Catalans in turn act rather like their oppressors. There are groups supporting Vlachs, Slavs and Albanians in Western Europe and America, although these groups too have something of the bitterness of the Catalans. Fundamentalist support for beleaguered Muslim fragments in Europe is growing in powerful, wealthy and dangerous quarters in the Middle East. It may be time for the Greek government to reverse the long-standing and largely successful policy of neglect and contempt towards minorities in favour of a more conciliatory policy. A few street signs, the odd language course and a less biassed attitude in historical works would help. At the moment supporters of ethnic fragments are abused, there is hysteria over Macedonia, and interference by foreigners over minority matters is hotly resented. There are minority cultural associations and these seem harmless and uncontroversial outlets that might actually help the Greek nationalists by reducing fragments to the comparatively trivial world of folklore.

The Greeks cannot both ignore their own fragments and expect us to recognise Greek fragments outside Hellas. The essential right of the citizen of every state to practise the religion and speak the language of his or her choice has to be respected. In spite of the strength of Orthodoxy Greece has a fairly good record of tolerance to Catholics and Protestants, Jews and Muslims.[23] In language matters their record is less impressive, but the minority languages have survived and perhaps deserve some kind of encouragement.[24]

Macedonia

What's in a name? The name Macedonia is thought to threaten the peace of Europe and the world. Thus perhaps names do matter and demand some explanation. The Makedones, an ancient name, first found in Herodotus, were a tribe living to the north of Classical Greece.[1] They were ruled by a king and in this and other respects did not conform to the norm of the Greek city state. In the Persian wars the Macedonians sided with the Persians; in the Peloponnesian wars they supported both sides. After a difficult period at the beginning of the fourth century Philip ascended the throne and brought the whole of Greece under his sway. The Athenian orator Demosthenes mocked at the barbarian ways of Philip and his son Alexander, but it was as the standard-bearer of Greek civilisation that Alexander the Great with a copy of Homer under his pillow led his armies as far east as the Punjab.[2]

Alexander died in 323 BC, and for the next two hundred years his successors fought over the remains of his empire. The Romans became involved in a series of wars against the rulers of Macedon and eventually in 146 BC, almost by accident, found themselves the rulers of the southern half of the Balkan peninsula. Civil wars were won and lost in battles near the borders of modern Macedonia and within the boundaries of the Roman province of Macedonia, a squat square bloc of land to the north of Classical Greece. The emperor Augustus defeated Cleopatra, the last remaining descendant of Alexander's successors, at

Actium in 31 BC, and during his subsequent reign through
steady and difficult campaigns the Roman frontier was
moved as far north as the Danube. For the next two
hundred years the Danube frontier remained safe, and
under Trajan the Romans moved further north to encompass much of modern Romania.

After nearly two centuries of peace trouble began on the
Danube frontier in the reign of Marcus Aurelius. Under
Roman imperial rule Greece and Macedonia had stag-
nated. Plutarch who came from northern Greece and the
Apostle Paul who visited towns in Macedonia are poor
substitutes for Plato and Philip. Happy is the land without
history, and Gibbon thought that the age of the Antonines
was such an age, but probably not for Macedonia. Plutarch
suggests depopulation and Paul demoralisation.[3]

Worse was to follow. In the four hundred years following
the death of Marcus Aurelius in 180 AD the Danube
frontier was frequently to buckle, never actually to break.
There were disasters like the defeat and death of the
Emperor Valens at Adrianople in 271. The Empire was
divided and subdivided with the main dividing line between East and West running through the formerly united
province of Illyricum roughly corresponding to modern
Yugoslavia. Macedonia lay generally in the Eastern half
of the Empire. Its inhabitants would have Greek as an
official language and many of them would speak it. Further to the north along the Danube frontier and to the west
opposite the Italian coast and even in the interior in places
like Scupi (Skopje) Latin would be the official language.
Native languages like Illyrian in the western Balkans and
Thracian in the eastern Balkans would still be spoken, and
in the case of Illyrian are still spoken today, since Illyrian
is almost certainly the ancestor of modern Albanian. The
ethnic picture is further confused by the presence of a large
number of invaders, mostly Germans, but some of Asiatic

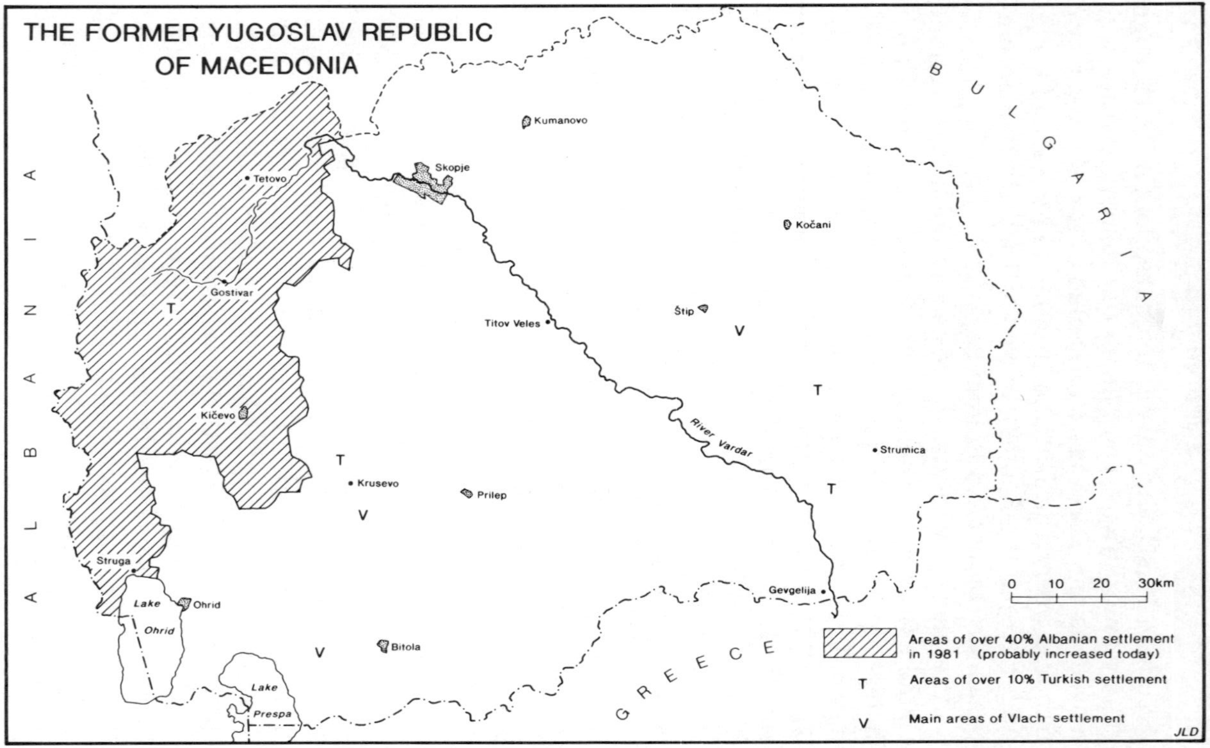
THE FORMER YUGOSLAV REPUBLIC OF MACEDONIA
ALBANIA
BULGARIA
GREECE
Kumanovo
Skopje
Tetovo
Gostivar
Kičevo
Kočani
Štip
Titov Veles
River Vardar
Strumica
Krusevo
Prilep
Struga
Ohrid
Lake Ohrid
Bitola
Lake Prespa
Gevgelija
T
V
0 10 20 30km
Areas of over 40% Albanian settlement in 1981 (probably increased today)
T Areas of over 10% Turkish settlement
V Main areas of Vlach settlement
JLD

Map 8

origin, who were let in within the confines of the Empire as mercenaries or unreliable allies.

With the collapse of the Western Empire in the fifth century pressure from Germanic tribes against the Eastern Empire eased slightly, and in the sixth century Justinian, a Latin-speaker from the Scupi area, felt strong enough to try to reconquer the West. He succeeded in restoring Italy, north Africa and southern Spain to imperial control, but except in parts of Italy his reconquests were transitory, and he weakened the resistance of the Eastern Empire to the next wave of invaders, the Slavs. Justinian's historian Procopius records the beginnings of Slav infiltration as sombre interludes in his account of triumphs in the West.[4]

The Slavs radically changed the ethnic composition of the Balkans in general and Macedonia in particular. Macedonia now needs defining, and we may take as a rough-and-ready definition the territory comprising the Greek province of this name, the former Yugoslav province which so controversially is trying to assert its right to this name, and the small section of Bulgaria to the west of the Struma river, usually known as Pirin Macedonia. Such an area is different from the Roman province and the area ruled by the pre-Roman Macedonian kings. The latter rarely stretched as far north and the former never did. With the invasion of the Slavs there was no Macedonia. There is no evidence of any Slav adopting the name or of the Byzantines preserving it for the small section of land around Salonica which remained loyal to Constantinople.[5] The name only re-emerges as a theme of the recovering Empire in the ninth century and, since the interior of the Balkans was not recovered until the eleventh century, Macedonia was originally only a small theme occupying an area roughly akin to western Thrace in modern Greece.

For four centuries the Slavs were the rulers of most of

modern Macedonia with Byzantine rule only strong along the coast. The Slavs occupied much of the rest of modern Greece as well, but left fewer permanent traces of their occupation, although especially in the west place names attest their presence. Slav was still spoken in the Peloponnese as late as the thirteenth century. If there was a rule that possession of land in 793 should determine who owned it in 1993, Greece would have few European possessions but would rule almost the whole of Turkey. Of course there is no such rule, and yet many Balkan wrangles appear to revolve round the question of who occupied the land first. Here the Greeks try and trump 793 AD with 493 BC when clearly there were no Slavs and much of Macedonia was occupied by Greek-speakers.

But of course the game is an absurd one. Under its rules much of England would be handed over to the Welsh and the United States to the Red Indians. Australia would be reclaimed by the Aborigines, and South Africa would pass neither to the Afrikaaners, nor to the Bantu, but to the Hottentots. In the Balkans politicians and historians continue to try and play the game of who got where first, especially in areas like Kosovo and Transylvania, where there are few historical records and plenty of prejudice in a mixed population. In Macedonia the game is more complicated because there are more players. The Greeks have a claim to their area because of their occupation before the Slav invasion and after the Byzantine occupation at the beginning of the eleventh century. This resulted in two centuries of Byzantine rule until the Fourth Crusade in 1204. The next two hundred years saw Macedonia initially divided between the Second Bulgarian Empire and the Latins, a brief period of Byzantine rule again, the short-lived conquest of the Serbian Nemanjid dynasty and then the arrival of the Ottoman Turks.

Macedonia was one of the first areas that the Turks

conquered in Europe and one of the last they surrendered. The Balkan wars of 1912 and 1913 divided the province between Serbia, Bulgaria and Greece with Bulgaria as loser in the second of these wars getting much the smallest share. On the wrong side in the First World War Bulgaria suffered further minor losses of territory after 1918 while Serbia, now enlarged into Yugoslavia, saw her possession of northern Macedonia confirmed. In the Second World War Bulgaria briefly occupied Yugoslav Macedonia (and Greek western Thrace), but the defeat of the Axis meant a return to the frontiers established after the First World War. Tito's new Yugoslavia was less dominated by the Serbs, and Macedonia gained some degree of autonomy in it as a separate province.[6]

Macedonia was also given a separate language. The status of this language is almost as difficult as the history of the land in which it is spoken. It is difficult to divide the South Slav languages or for that matter any Slav languages into neat self-contained units. Rather there is a language continuum from Slovenia in the north west to Bulgaria in the south east, whereby each village can understand the village next to it, but Slovene speakers are totally unintelligible to Bulgarian speakers and vice versa.[7] In Macedonia the Slav language is more like Bulgarian than it is like Serbo-Croatian. When he recognised Macedonia Tito gave formal notice that the language spoken in the province was distinct from Serbian, although in doing so he made sure that the dialect he standardised into a language incorporated forms that were different from Bulgarian. Nevertheless Macedonian as it is now written and spoken in the former Yugoslav province of Macedonia is easily intelligible to the Bulgarians and to the Slav-speakers of northern Greece. In 1878 the treaty of San Stefano awarded most of Yugoslav and Greek Macedonia to the Bulgarians for this reason.

Bulgaria in some sense ruled Macedonia from the eighth to the tenth century and then again in the thirteenth. Exponents of a Macedonian role as distinct from a Bulgarian are able to show that Samuel, the last great emperor before the Byzantine reconquest, was in some sense a Macedonian. The centre of his empire was the area around lakes Ohrid and Prespa, and he ruled much of northern Greece. Eastern Bulgaria on the other hand had already been conquered by the Byzantines. It is true that Samuel's great opponent, the restorer of the fortunes of Byzantium, was known as Basil the Bulgarslayer, but Byzantine historians are notoriously unreliable in describing the racial origins of their opponents. The founders of the second Bulgarian empire were described as Vlachs.

Serbia's occupation of Macedonia in the Middle Ages was much more ephemeral. The Nemanjid kings steadily extended their power southwards, but it was not until Stephan Dušan's reign that they gained all of Macedonia apart from Salonica. Dušan, whose empire reached as far as the Isthmus of Corinth, aspired to be Emperor of Constantinople. His court was Byzantine and he stressed that he ruled many races. On his death in 1355 his empire quickly fell to pieces. Both Serbian and Bulgarian lays tell of the exploits of the heroes like Marko Kraljević who ruled briefly over the fragments. Byzantine sources make fun of the multi-ethnic nature of some of these leaders.[8]

In the nineteenth century as in the fourteenth Macedonia was a medley of different races – so much so that the term 'Macedoine' was coined in cookery to describe a mixture of fruit embedded in a jelly. Many of its inhabitants spoke more than one language, most wrote none. Loyalties were frequently decided on religious grounds with the two main contenders being the Exarchists supporting the Bulgarian church and the Patriarchists supporting the Greek church. The Serbs were weakly represented. Other racial or religious groups were the largely Muslim Albanians, the Slav-speaking Muslim Pomaks, the Vlachs, usually but not always associated with the Greeks, the almost unrecognised Gypsies, and of course a large number of Turks. There was a strong colony of Spanish-speaking Jews in Salonica, and a fair collection of Armenians. Supporters of the Exarchist church could be found as far south as Kastoria and Edessa, supporters of the Patriarchists as far north as Strumica and Prilep, and the drawing of any boundary would have been bound to upset one or other party.

The boundaries that were in fact drawn were not ideal. The treaty of San Stefano in 1878 gave practically everything to Bulgaria, but this treaty was revoked and under the treaty of Berlin in the same year Macedonia remained nominally Turkish, though hotly disputed by wandering bands of brigands representing the various nationalities. For the Greeks this period of history is called the struggle for Macedonia. They wished to extend their frontiers as far north as possible. The treaty of Berlin had given them Thessaly, but there were still many people of Greek language and sentiment to the north of Thessaly. Unfortunately these were mixed up with people from many other races. The Bulgarians also used the name Macedonia in their organisation, the Internal Macedonian Revolutionary Organisation, abbreviated to IMRO, which continued its violent existence after the First World War. Some members of this organisation believed or pretended to believe in an independent Macedonia, but there was not a great deal of support for this idea. Goce Delčev does seem to have been a genuine fighter for the oppressed of all races. In the Ilinden rising of 1902 which started in the largely Vlach town of Kruševo he had some support among the Vlachs.[9] The idea of a separate Macedonian nation was also favoured by the Serbian geographer Cjivić, but this was probably part of a campaign to do down Bulgarian claims.[10]

The frontiers drawn after the Balkan wars and modified after the First World War clearly favoured Serbia and Greece at the expense of Bulgaria. Others to lose out were the Albanians, left in large numbers in western Macedonia as well as Kosovo, the minor ethnic groups, and anyone in Macedonia who harboured ideas of independence. Some Greeks were left north of the border, but a series of population exchanges largely rectified this anomaly, and a policy of neglect has greatly diminished the numbers of Slav-speakers in Greece.

The Yugoslav province of Macedonia has been less neglectful of its minorities. Though vigorously promoting Macedonian, the state has allowed some educational rights to the Albanians and Turks, the two largest minorities. In the 1981 census 19.8 per cent of the population were said to be Albanian, 4.5 per cent Turkish, but both figures are probably too small. Patriotic pressure to declare oneself a Macedonian may have put up the number of Macedonians (67 per cent). A high birth rate as in Kosovo and a certain amount of immigration from Kosovo has increased the number of Albanians. The number of Turks has probably decreased because some have registered themselves as Muslims. Muslims, Gypsies, Vlachs and Serbs make up most of the remaining 9.7 per cent.[11]

Greek politicians seize upon these figures and exaggerate them to show the impossibility of Yugoslav Macedonia existing as a state of its own. The number of Albanians is increased to include all the non-Macedonians. Vlachs who are regarded as honorary Greeks, are said to exist in large numbers. It is conveniently forgotten that in 1918 Greek Macedonia had less than 50 per cent of Greek-speakers. Of all the former Yugoslav provinces only Slovenia is ethnically homogeneous with according to the 1981 statistics a 90 per cent Slovene population. Croatia is 75 per cent Croatian, Montenegro 68.5 per cent Montenegrin. Serbia, including Kosovo and the Voivodina, 66.4 per cent Serbian.[12] Macedonia is not as fragmented as Bosnia, which in 1981 was 39 per cent Muslim. Of Macedonia's minorities neither the Albanians nor the Turks are likely to receive a great deal of support from Albania or Turkey. The Albanian minority is largely concentrated in western Macedonia, and we do not have as in Bosnia the patchwork pattern whereby there are large pockets of Serbs in the north of Bosnia and the adjoining Krajina area of Croatia, separated from the main mass of Serbs. It must be a help to Macedonia that the Serb minority there is comparatively small.

In spite of these factors in Macedonia's favour, politicians and journalists have consistently predicted a forthcoming disaster in Macedonia on a scale that would make the horrific events in Bosnia seem quite tame. At present Macedonia lies in limbo. The Serbian government finds it convenient for breaking sanctions. The Albanian party has a place in the cabinet. The Greeks have conducted an expensive and fairly successful campaign to prevent the state of Macedonia being recognised, at any rate under this name. Balkan pundits were slow to see trouble brewing in Bosnia, and slow to see the consequences of the recognition of Croatia and Slovenia. It is perhaps understandable that they should be so nervous and cautious about Macedonia. This fear and this care have played into the hands of the Greek propaganda machine, and so finally we come to the name Macedonia.

Greece has been nervous for a long time about its northern borders. It was lucky to get them in 1913, lucky to hold on to them in 1918. The Germans took away some of northern Greece during the Second World War, and after this war the Communists threatened to do the same. A Macedonian state was part of Communist propaganda, although not many Greek Communists believe in it. Many Slav-speakers were on the Communist side. Greece still has a small Slav minority. So Greece is understandably nervous, and can point out that neither history nor linguistics really suggest that a Macedonian nation exists. On the other hand, people in Yugoslavia have for the past fifty years been persuaded that they do belong to just such a nation. History books and grammars have been written to establish the validity of this nation and its language, and to prove that 'Macedonia' and 'Macedonian' are the names of this nation and its language. It seems a little difficult to start rewriting these books.

It is not difficult to find vaguely similar cases where part of one country has the same name or a name like that of another. Brittany, New England and the Dutch province of Luxembourg are three examples of names that cause no trouble whatsoever. They are not quite similar to Macedonia, where, as it would seem to the Greeks, the whole of a new state is adopting the name of part of another and, in laying claim to this name, is also claiming the actual province. This is what the Greeks fear, and it is in vain that the Macedonian government protests its unwillingness to make the latter claim, which it would be powerless to achieve.

Yugoslav Macedonia cannot live in limbo for ever. Most of its future options seem fairly bleak. A marriage, either forced or voluntary, to the rump of Yugoslavia would produce another Kosovo with Macedonian as well as Albanian resistance and objections to the reimposition of Communism. Partition is a dirty word after Bosnia, although partition of Macedonia would be relatively simple, perhaps following the pattern of the partition of Poland in the eighteenth century. Serbia would take the north, Albania the west, Bulgaria the east and Greece the south. Skopje, like Sarajevo, would not be easy to divide.[13] A division would have been easier in 1913 if the Balkan wars had followed a different course. If the Bulgarians had not borne the brunt of the attack on the Turkish positions in Thrace they might have taken eastern Macedonia and kept it. If the Greeks had not been so busy getting first to Salonica they might have occupied Bitola.

But we cannot write history now by rewriting 1913. A partition does not make sense now. Few inhabitants of Yugoslav Macedonia want to join communist Serbia, backward Albania, Greek-speaking Greece or even the relatively stable Bulgaria, and these countries have enough economic and political problems on their hands without adding fractious Macedonia to them. The only part of Macedonia that might be attractive is the area around lakes Ohrid and Prespa, an area of great tourist potential with historic buildings and beautiful scenery. This area is close geographically to Greece and Albania, which share the lakes, is attached to Bulgaria by historical and cultural links and has an odd connection with Serbia because many of the buildings along the lake are, or used to be, owned by workers' associations in places like Belgrade. The rest of Macedonia is poor and barren. There has been massive emigration from the villages to cities like Skopje, full of soulless high-rise flats, although some picturesque squalor survived the earthquake of 1963.

So it looks like Macedonia for the Macedonians, a cry uttered by Gladstone in spite of his Classical training and Bulgarian sympathies.[14] The West, too quick to recognise Slovenia, too slow to see problems arising in Bosnia, has blown hot and cold over Macedonia for fear of offending Greek sensitivity. In April 1992 when I asked for some cheese in a Salonica restaurant the waiter would not give it to me unless I said Macedonia was Greek. This chapter would ensure the confiscation of my cheese. It is possible to think of ingenious ways round the problem for the emergent state, of, as it were, having one's cheese and eating it. The authorities in Skopje could model themselves on Greece, which calls itself Hellas, or Albania, which calls itself Shqiperia, and have one name for internal use and another for external. Macedonia would work for inhabitants of the former province of Yugoslavia, but some name like Dardania (classical and rather grand with Trojan as well as Roman associations) or Skopia (the rather contemptuous Greek designation at the moment) would have to be adopted for such bodies as the United Nations. Or there could be some title like Vardar Macedonia or Slav Macedonia or northern Macedonia, although these probably would not work. The Greeks used to call southern Albania northern Epirus. They have now dropped this claim, although there is still tension in this area. In Korcë in 1993 I saw an official-looking notice in Greek referring apparently to eastern Albania as western Macedonia, but this may be an aberration. Greece cannot and does not lay claim to Yugoslav Macedonia. One can occasionally find in Skopje or Bitola or the border villages an old person who speaks Greek, usually either a Vlach or a refugee from the Greek civil war, but there is no Greek minority as there is in southern Albania. Yet logically, if northern Epirus is a compliment to the Greeks, why should northern Macedonia be an insult? The present acronym FYROM (Former Yugoslav Republic of Macedonia) does not seem a very promising starter.

And yet the Greeks are easily insulted, as my waiter showed. We probably have to risk the insult and come down on the anti-Greek side, as this chapter has tried to show. Of course Alexander the Great was not a Slav, of course Greek literature and culture are great boons to

mankind, of course *pace* Gibbon Byzantium and the Greek
Orthodox church were great bulwarks in the defence of
civilisation, of course the Greeks played a leading part in
the Macedonian struggle against the Turks, of course the
Greeks were on the right side in two Balkan wars and two
world wars, and of course in the civil war the Greeks fought
nobly to defend freedom and democracy, two concepts they
had invented. None of these certainties alter the fact that,
to the north of frontiers first erected in 1913 and only
altered briefly by the Germans in the Second World War,
there is a population which has very little to do with Greece
but whose best chance of freedom and democracy probably
lies in an independent Macedonian nation, however shal-
lowly rooted in history such a nation is.

In my chapter on the Vlach Diaspora I drew attention
to a family from the Macedonian village of Nižepolje who
had emigrated to Australia, taking with them Serb,
Bulgarian or Macedonian names according to the time of
emigration. Their mother, who had lived for the first
twelve years of her life under the Ottoman Empire, spoke
Greek and Vlach and got on well with her Albanian
neighbours. Indeed everyone both in Nižepolje and in
Australia seemed to get on well with everyone else, and
the village could be a beacon of hope that Macedonia
under any kind of name could be a genuinely multi-
cultural society.

Yugoslavia was a multi-cultural society. Thanks to the
strong arm of Tito it nearly succeeded, but in 1992 it failed,
and its shattered fragments may seem a tribute to the
impossibility of the dream, although they are also a tribute
to its desirability. Macedonia was also an attempt at a
multi-cultural society. Here the fragments are just about
holding together, although the cement that binds them is
a rather unreliable mixture of propaganda and myth. The
Macedonian language has been created, some rather misty

history involving Tsar Samuel, probably a Bulgarian, and Alexander the Great, almost certainly a Greek, has been invented, and the name Macedonia has been adopted. Do we try to destroy these myths or live with them?[15]

9

Kosovo

On the map Kosovo is a small rather neat rhombus wedged in between Montenegro to the west, Albania to the south west, Macedonia to the south east and the ever enveloping Serbia to the north and east. In shape and size and population, but not in history, it curiously resembles another rhomboid-like state, Montenegro, and in shape, size, population and history it vaguely resembles another troubled province, Northern Ireland. Unlike Northern Ireland its boundaries are sharply defined. Between it and Macedonia, Albania and Montenegro high mountain ranges, rising to well over two thousand metres, debar entry or exit. In April 1988, trying to reach Montenegro from Macedonia, I made a long detour through snow-covered passes to get to Prizren to the south of Kosovo and travelled through a flat valley to Peć, only to be told that there was no way west or north through the snow, and that I would have to travel back to Kosovo Polje in the east of the province and then into Serbia in order to get into Montenegro.

Between Kosovo and southern Serbia the mountains, though high, are less impregnable, and our car got through without any difficulty, as it did through what seemed a fairly low range of hills in the centre of the province. This area in the centre is known as Drenica after the river that runs through it. The Drenica is a tributary of the Sitnica which is a tributary of the Ibar which is a tributary of the Morava which is a tributary of the Danube which runs into the Black Sea. Also in Drenica are the head waters of the Bistrica which runs into the White Drin which runs into the Black Drin to emerge into the Adriatic, and the head waters of the Sazlija which becomes the Neromidka which becomes the Vardar which, known as the Axios, flows into the Aegean.

Rivers run innocently, men less so. Kosovo is a central square in the chequerboard of Balkan geography, and as in chess where the four central squares are hotly disputed, so in history Kosovo has been the scene of numerous battles. The most famous of these battles was fought between the Serbs and Turks on 28 June 1389. Sultan Murad of the Turks was assassinated just before the battle, Prince Lazar of the Serbs was executed just after it. These facts are at any rate certain in a story etched into Serbian memory by a series of epic lays in which history tends to be replaced by legend. The result of the battle is in doubt. It seems like a double checkmate. In the West bells were initially rung for what seemed a heroic victory. Serbian songs see the battle as a heroic defeat. Turkish sources are paradoxically ambiguous.[1] We see battles too easily in chess terms of winning and losing, black and white. Probably at Kosovo there were men of a variety of races on both sides and, both before and after the battle Kosovo and Southern Serbia, they were ruled by leaders who owed some kind of allegiance to the Turks.

In 1448 two of the last remaining defenders of the Balkans, the Hungarian Hunyadi and the Albanian Scanderbeg agreed to meet on the plains of Kosovo, but Sultan Murad's great-grandson, also called Murad, checkmated them by arriving early and routing Hunyadi before Scanderbeg had time to arrive. We hear less of this battle in Serbian lays, although the two battles were probably confused. After the first battle Lazar's son Stephen kept control of Kosovo, which together with northern Serbia he

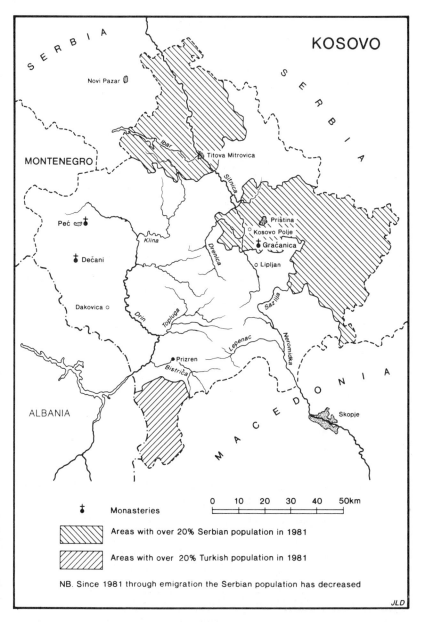

KOSOVO

SERBIA

Novi Pazar

MONTENEGRO

SERBIA

Ibar

Titova Mitrovica

Sitnica

Peć

Klina

Priština

Kosovo Polje

Gračanica

Dečani

Drenica

Lipljan

Dakovica

Drin

Topluga

Saz Ilja

Neromidka

Lepenac

Prizren

Bistrica

ALBANIA

MACEDONIA

Skopje

♱♠ Monasteries

◢◣ Areas with over 20% Serbian population in 1981

◢◣ Areas with over 20% Turkish population in 1981

NB. Since 1981 through emigration the Serbian population has decreased

0 10 20 30 40 50km

JLD

Map 9

handed over intact to his successor, George Brancović. This ruler, who finally lost Kosovo to the Turks, played rather a dubious part in the second battle, a part which may have unfairly blackened the reputation of his grandfather Vuk Brancović in legends about the first.

After some hundred years of semi-independence Kosovo finally became Turkish and remained so for over four hundred and fifty years. There is still a sizeable Turkish minority in the province. In the seventeenth century the Austro-Hungarian Empire began expanding into the now enfeebled Ottoman Empire. There was another battle which the Hapsburgs won in 1688. Austria was anxious to keep Kosovo as a white square between the two black squares of Montenegro and Serbia,[2] and even for a short time took control of the Sandjak of Novi Pazar just north of Kosovo, but Turkey's defeat in the Balkan war of 1912 meant the division of Kosovo and the Sandjak between the two orthodox Slav states, united in Yugoslavia after the First World War. When the Serbian armies retook Kosovo after a fourth battle they kissed the ground in homage to their past.

Unfortunately, by the time of this reconquest, Kosovo was largely inhabited by Albanians. This fact was recognised during the Second World War when the Axis carved up Yugoslavia and gave most of Kosovo and some of Macedonia to a puppet Albania. It was recognised in a half-hearted way under Tito, when Kosovo was briefly given autonomous status, as was Voivoidina, within the Republic of Serbia. This status was too little for Albanian nationalists who demanded and are demanding a full republic akin to Montenegro, and too much for full-blooded Serbs, who in the present wave of hardline chauvinism have rescinded Kosovo's autonomy.[3] At the moment the growing Albanian birthrate means that the Serbs are outnumbered in Kosovo by nearly 6 to 1, and the growing nationalist mood of Serbia means that the majority are ruled as a subject people by this thin minority.

It is possible, though unfashionable, to have some sympathy for Serb claims to Kosovo. Literature in the shape of the epic lays, and religion in the shape of the magnificent churches of Dečani, Gračanica and Peć show a strong Serbian presence in the area during the fourteenth century. The Kosovo lays became famous because of the work of Milman Parry who showed that they shared stylistic features in common with the *Iliad* and the *Odyssey*, features which result from the poems being originally sung by illiterate bards.[4] More recent Homeric scholarship has suggested that there is a pattern and purpose behind the *Iliad* and the *Odyssey*, well beyond the capability of illiterate bards, but in fact it is possible to trace in the Kosovo legends a kind of philosophical thread. Prince Lazar is offered the choice of a heavenly kingdom or an earthly kingdom. He chooses the heavenly kingdom, loses the battle, but leaves his fellow Serbs an eternal legacy enshrined in the great churches and monasteries of the area.

History works on a rather less lofty level. It is extremely difficult to use Homer or the Kosovo lays as historical evidence, but there is not a great deal of other evidence for the history of Kosovo. In pre-Roman times it was inhabited by the Dardanians, like the Illyrians further west a thorn in the side of the Macedonian kingdom, but probably of a different race from either Illyrians or Macedonians. The Romans after fighting their way to the Danube frontier made strenuous and largely unexcavated efforts through roads and towns to link the Danube to the Adriatic coast. Priština is on the site of ancient Theranda, Lipljan preserves the name of ancient Ulpiana.

When Diocletian split his empire Kosovo and Bosnia both fell somewhere between East and West, now passing to one half, now to another. This ambiguity, later reflected

in a divided religious loyalty, was to have terrible consequences for both provinces. When the Western Empire fell,
most of modern Yugoslavia, including Kosovo, remained
in the still vigorous Eastern Empire, although as previously pointed out there were still Latin-speakers in this
eastern section. It could be maintained that the oldest and
therefore the best qualified inhabitants of Kosovo are the
Latin-speaking Vlachs, undoubtedly present in medieval
and even modern times.[5] In the sixth century the Slav
invasions began, and we have almost no accounts of the
history of Kosovo. In the eastern Balkans the Bulgarians
created a strong kingdom that challenged Byzantium. The
Serbs in the west were less united and less independent.
Kosovo would have been under Bulgarian control for some
of this dark age until at the beginning of the eleventh
century Basil the Bulgarslayer again recovered all the
land south of the Danube. Kosovo and Serbia would then
have remained under nominal Byzantine control for two
hundred years.

With the Fourth Crusade and the rise of the Second
Bulgarian or Vlach Empire Kosovo passed for ever from
Byzantine rule. Initially Bulgarian, it soon fell under the
sway of the powerful Serb Nemanjid dynasty. Under this
dynasty, bloodthirsty but pious, Serbia at last came into
its own. Its founder, Stephen Nemanja, had his capital at
Raš, near Novi Pazar, but united the zupanate of Raška to
that of Zeta, which was roughly equivalent to modern
Montenegro. His elder son obtained the title of king from
the Pope, while his younger son Sava became archbishop
of a Serbian orthodox church with its centre at Peć in
Kosovo. Successive kings drove the frontier southwards.
The capital was briefly at Priština, the modern capital of
Kosovo, but Stephen Uros II (1282-1321) moved it to
Skopje. Under Stephen Dušan (1321-1355) the Serbian
Empire reached its zenith with Kosovo and Macedonia at

its centre. Like the Byzantine Empire, whose art and culture it aped, Dušan's empire was a multi-racial one. The royal family by frequent dynastic marriages were linked to other rulers of the Balkans.

Dušan's aim was to found a new dynasty at Constantinople, but he died one year after the first establishment of the Turks in Europe, and with startling rapidity his empire fell to pieces, the Turks being the chief gainers. His son, Stephen Uros V, lived until 1371, the year in which the Turks defeated a united Slav army at the battle of the Maritsa, but long before his death the Serbian Empire existed only in name with its territory disputed by feuding warlords. Many of these warlords became vassals of the Turks, notably Marko Kraljević of Prilep and Tsar Lazar of Kosovo fame. Lazar only revolted when the Sultan demanded that he take part in a Turkish campaign, and Lazar's son did actually take part in such a campaign, fighting heroically with a Serbian contingent against Tamburlaine in the battle of Ankara of 1402.

Such historic facts tend to be forgotten in glorious legends, magnified by nationalist pride. However, history does show a strong Serbian presence in Kosovo and even in Macedonia, under the Nemanjids. Marko Kraljević did live in Prilep, Macedonia. It is true that he is also a hero of Bulgarian songs, and that some of his exploits remind us of the Byzantine epic of Digenis Akrites.[6] William of Tyre in the thirteenth century spoke ill of Serbs in Bitola, and Byzantine chroniclers mention Serbs in Greece.[7]

When the Turks took control of Kosovo after the second battle in 1448, we have the first proper records of who was living in the disputed territory. Unfortunately Albanian and Serbian historians dispute the findings of these records.[8] The Turks did not distinguish their subjects into separate races, and the names given can be interpreted in different ways. In fact ethnic identity was never a very important factor in medieval times. The Byzantine Empire was a multi-ethnic state, a fact that Dušan recognised when in his challenge for the throne of Constantinople he called himself Emperor and Autocrat of the Serbs, Greeks, Bulgarians and Albanians. Even the patriotic lays of Kosovo find it hard to disguise the fact that on the fatal day there were both Serbs and Albanians fighting on both sides, although this fact is not part of official Serbian or Albanian history.[9]

National feeling was not and probably is not as important as religious feeling. Even the Turks distinguished those of the true faith from infidels. Conversions to Islam were frequent in areas such as Bosnia and Albania where loyalties were divided between Orthodoxy and Catholicism. There were economic motives for such conversions, and the presence in the area of the Bogomil heresy was another factor. Thanks to the patriarchate of Peć Orthodoxy was strong in Kosovo, but in 1691 the Patriarch Arsenje III organised a great emigration from Kosovo to settle in southern Hungary. Whatever the ethnic composition of Kosovo before this date, it is clear that after it Albanian Muslims were in the majority.

By 1691 the Ottoman Empire was clearly in decline. Austrian armies were generally victorious, but had by the treaty of Karlovitz in 1699 only been awarded northern Croatia. In the eighteenth century economic factors led to large-scale emigration from the Balkans into central Europe.[10] Tensions between Catholicism and Orthodoxy made the Serbs less eager to rise against the Turks. The Serbian religious position was weakened by the decision to abolish the patriarchate of Peć in 1766 and to put the Serbian church under the control of the Greeks.

Early nineteenth-century nationalism revolted against this decision. The Serbs found a new defender in the Russians, both Slav and Orthodox. The great Serbian scholar Vuk Karaždić amazingly succeeded in welding together a number of disparate dialects into a common literary tongue. It was perhaps unfortunate that this literary language was based on the language of the Kosovo lays, and that both the religious and literary heart of modern Serbia was thus to be found in a province to which otherwise they had little linguistic claim. Greece had similar religious problems with Constantinople, but could at any rate look to an alternative linguistic and literary heritage based on Athens.

It took almost a hundred years before Serbia, which had gained some kind of autonomy for the area and around Belgrade in 1815, reached the sacred soil of Kosovo in 1912. The Serbs were helped by the Russians, hindered by the Austrians. They were helped by some sympathy in England and France for emergent small nations, hindered by the behaviour of rival royal dynasties, as violent and treacherous as the Nemanjids, but not as powerful. Nevertheless gallant little Serbia won and still wins some support from contemporary politicians and modern historians, even though it was Serbia with her Austrian enemies and Russian friends who brought about the First World War. In this war the Serbs after a brave initial resistance were easily crushed by superior manpower and had to fight their way through Kosovo and Albania to a safe refuge in Corfu. This fighting march in which the Serbs abandoned their heavy artillery but preserved their religious relics did not improve Serb-Albanian relations.

Transferred from Corfu to Salonica the Serbian army took part in the final Allied advance, and was rewarded for being on the right side by being transformed into greater Yugoslavia, gaining territory in the process from Austria, Hungary, Bulgaria and even in the Kosovo area from Albania. The inter-war years were not happy ones with Croatian and Macedonian nationalism resentful of Serbian rule. King Alexander, a Serb, eventually assassinated in 1934 by a combination of revolutionary movements, strove in vain for Yugoslav unity, even dividing the country in 1929 into banovine which cut across ethnic divisions. Thus Kosovo, though mainly in Zetska, which also included Montenegro, was also in Vardarska, a larger Macedonia, and Moravska or Eastern Serbia.

In 1941 the Axis after a lightning invasion set about dismembering Yugoslavia. Kosovo became part of an Italian-dominated Albania. There was a Scanderbeg division formed to fight against Yugoslav resistance, which after the Italian collapse in 1943 soon proved superior. Tito's stand against the German and Italian occupation proved popular with all sections of the community. He made some concessions to nationalist feeling by making Macedonia a separate republic and giving Kosovo limited autonomy. The break with Stalin in 1948 meant a break with Albania, with whom Yugoslavia had been previously on very good terms, so much so that it almost looked as if Albania might become an additional Yugoslav republic.

Economic difficulties in 1968 led to riots in Kosovo. More favourable treatment accorded to the region led to resentment against it. This resentment had unfortunate consequences. Prosperous and hard-working Slovenes objected to the amount of money in the federal budget given to what they saw as the feckless population of the southern part of the country. Eventually they carried their objections to the point of secession. This secession was painless, that of Croatia less so. The beleaguered Communist regime in Serbia, faced with external isolation and internal resentment, rode hard, and for a time successfully, on a wave of pro-Serb chauvinism. Kosovo is now ruled by the Serbs in much the same way as the South African government used to rule that country before the release of Nelson Mandela.

The comparison is not an exact one. The Albanians do have voting rights, but choose not to use them. They used to be able to go and enjoy education at the University of Priština, but classes are now held only in Serbian, and the Albanians boycott the university. Hyperinflation and a low budget cause most misery among the poor, and the Albanians have always been poor. Kosovo now bears all the hallmarks of a police state.

Of course, right is not all on one side. Truth is very rarely pure and never simple. It is natural that the Serbs in Kosovo dislike the Albanians. Events in both world wars hardly encouraged friendship. There is a long record of hostility between Christianity and Islam in the Balkans, and the Albanians and Turks in Kosovo are Muslims. In Kosovo the Serbs can with some justification point to the barbaric institution of the blood feud, still strong here, having been less successfully stamped out than in Hoxha's Albania. The ready sympathy of progressive liberals in the West is naturally enlisted on behalf of the oppressed Albanian population of Kosovo. Such sympathy might not be so easily accorded if it was known that some families are so keen on male heirs that they pass off their girls as boys, thus condemning some unfortunate females to a life of masculine toil and enforced virginity.[10]

Above all the Serbs are in the unfortunate position of being a majority threatened with being turned into a minority. There is an analogy with Northern Ireland here, but not an exact one. Protestants outnumber Catholics in Ulster by roughly 2 to 1 under the present regime, but would be outnumbered by the same proportion if Northern Ireland became part of a United Ireland. Serbs outnumber Albanians by 5 to 1 in the whole of Serbia, including Kosovo and the Voivodina, but would be outnumbered by almost 6 to 1 if Kosovo became independent. If Kosovo were to join Albania the Serbs would of course be in a tiny minority, but here the parallel breaks down as both geography and economics make the idea of a United Albania a fairly unlikely one. The Albanian government has enough problems of its own without adding the running of a broken province to them. This province is detached from them by a high mountain barrier and forty-five years of isolation as a result of Hoxha's break with Tito. Albanians have mixed feelings for the Kosovars, even by a fine irony making jokes about them in the same way as the British make jokes about the Irish.

The Serbs like the Ulster Protestants have their national myth, Prince Lazar being a more romantic if less successful totem pole than William of Orange. The Kosovo Albanians have less history to sustain them. Scanderbeg, the only figure in Albanian history before the nineteenth century, did not play much part in the history of Kosovo apart from missing his appointment with Hunyadi. The first stirrings of Albanian independence came late in the nineteenth century and lacked unity of focus. The Albanians had three religions and their language lacked a common alphabet. Early advocates of Albanian independence often lived abroad, sometimes as officials of the Ottoman Empire. Many of the revolutionary movements of the Albanians were directed against independence from the Turks rather than for it, since Albanians led by their powerful beys preferred the Ottoman rule or the lack of it to being divided between Serbia, Montenegro, Bulgaria and Greece, all non-Islamic states.

It was, it is true, at Prizren in Kosovo that the first stirrings of Albanian independence were heard in 1878. Patriots gathered from inside and outside Albania to establish a league, quickly suppressed by the Turkish authorities. In this league there were more representatives from the Ghegs in the north than the Tosks in the south, and more enthusiasm for independence from Albanian regions outside modern Albania than those inside it. Albania's birth in the Balkans virtually co-incided with the liberation of Kosovo from the Turks, and both events were overtaken by the First World War in which both areas were occupied by foreign powers. In between the wars there were rapid changes of regime in Albania and complicated boundary nego-tiations between Yugoslavia and Albania. Any move-ment for the independence of Kosovo or its union with Albania stood little chance of wide recognition, espe-cially as Yugoslavia was faced by so many other schis-matic movements. In the Second World War one of the parties opposing the Communist Partisans was the Balli Kombëtar, hostile to the Italians, hostile to King Zog, but in favour of independence for Kosovo. Hoxha how-ever until 1948 was strongly under Yugoslav influence and then broke abruptly with Tito. Not surprisingly Kosovo did not feature very highly on either country's agenda.

Kosovo now stands high on the agenda of Balkan pun-dits, predicting doom and gloom in the near future. In Bosnia Serbs pursue a policy of ethnic cleansing, but it is hardly possible to do this in Kosovo without creating a desert. Against the run of propaganda Serbs claim that Muslims are killing Serbs in Bosnia and no doubt fear for their fellow countrymen in Kosovo, although very few Serbs have been killed. Albania is unlikely to take on the superior Serb army without provocation, but is unlikely to stand by idly if there is insurrection in Kosovo. Miracu-lously the Albanian majority have so far avoided violence in their resistance.

An independent Kosovo with a population of one and a half million is not a total impossibility. Slovenia and Macedonia are not much larger, Montenegro much smaller.[11] But Kosovo is economically poor, and the infra-structure is at the moment controlled by the Serbs. The two valleys of Kosovo and Metohia have potentially valu-able agricultural land, but the rapidly growing population means that it can hardly be self-sufficient. Recent events have deprived many young Kosovars from earning a living as gastarbeiter in Germany. The great Serbian monu-ments hardly bring in any tourists now, and it is difficult to see them doing so in the future.

One possible way forward would be for Kosovo to unite with another Balkan state. Montenegro has traditionally been the foe of the Albanians and the friend of the Serbs. Bosnia or what is left of it is not geographically contiguous to Kosovo, and apart from Islam the inhabitants of Sara-jevo have little in common with the Kosovars. Macedonia seems the best bet. If the two states united there would be a total population of three and half million inhabitants, of whom one and a half million would be Albanians and one and a half million would be Slavs of one kind or another. Such a state would be economically viable with better communications than either state on its own. It would share on the one hand a common Nemanjid and Orthodox history, on the other a long rule by Islam.

It is true that nation states with two different races have not been a great success. Belgium, Cyprus, Lebanon and Sri Lanka are hardly comforting examples. It is true that the Serbs, even buttressed by their fellow Orthodox Slavs, the Macedonians, would be reluctant to give up their hegemony in Kosovo. But we cannot go on fragmenting the Balkans for ever. Both Kosovo and Macedonia are full of tiny fragments, some of which have been discussed or mentioned, like the Vlachs on Mount Pelister, the Pomaks near Prilep, the Turks near Prizren. One can go on multi-plying examples; there are gypsy communities which claim Egyptian nationality, tin workers in Priština who have strange argots of their own, but we don't hear much about these fragments as they do realise that they must subordinate something of the part, and forget something of the past, to save the whole. Most of what was Yugoslavia does not seem to have learned this lesson.

Shattered Eagles

The two-headed eagle is the symbol of Byzantium. Because the Russian Imperial family was descended from the niece of the last Byzantine emperor, Imperial Russia too adopted the double eagle. By some strange heraldic quirk the Austro-Hungarian empire also had the double eagle as its crest. These two Empires were rivals in the Balkans, but both collapsed at the end of the First World War which their rivalry had started, and the only country today proudly to fly the double eagle on its flag is Albania, although Yeltsin's Russia is now making a belated claim to return to its former emblem.

Eagles are impressive symbols of empire. Rome conquered the Mediterranean with legions tramping behind eagles, and eighteen centuries later French soldiers followed eagle standards to carve out an empire for Napoleon. A double eagle should represent double authority, but in fact the Russian and Hapsburg empires were cruelly weakened by facing both ways, the former torn between Western liberalism and Slav mysticism, the latter forced by events in Germany to expand fatally into the Balkans. Both Tsar and Kaiser ruled a divided realm in a way that the first Caesars did not.

The Byzantine Empire, though often like its Ottoman successor facing dangers in East and West, was less fatally divided, but it is perhaps worth commenting on the origin of its double eagle, so relevant to the shattered Balkans and the battered fragments whose story we have been

Map 10

trying to tell. At the end of the third century the Roman Emperor Diocletian decided that the best way to rule his difficult empire was to divide it. The Roman Empire was easily divisible. Just before its inception it had been divided into a Western half ruled by Octavian and an Eastern half ruled by Antony. In the Western half most civilised people spoke a form of Latin, in the Eastern a form of Greek. After the battle of Actium in 31 BC, Augustus, as Octavian learnt to call himself, ruled both East and West, but the divisions between the Greek-speaking and Latin-speaking halves of the Empire remained and were reinforced as the Pax Romana strengthened both Latin and Greek as instruments of civilisation. Before the end of the second century after Christ the Empire was under attack along its northern frontiers. The third century was a chronicle of disasters. Diocletian, unfairly remembered as the persecutor of Christians, did much to restore order. By dividing the Empire he ensured that one part of the army could concentrate of the Rhine frontier, another on the Danube. But he introduced the double eagle.[2]

As in all boundary disputes (Bosnia, Ulster, India), the dividing line was difficult to draw. It is perhaps not wholly inappropriate that Diocletian should spend his declining days in the town called Split where his ruined palace, still surviving in a fragmented Yugoslavia, is in more than one way a monument to the thesis that 'divide' is not a synonym for 'impera'. In the fourth century frequent divisions of the Roman Empire are unfortunately reminiscent of recent boundary changes in Eastern Europe. Constantine reunited the Empire, adopted Christianity as its official religion, and at the council of Nicaea (AD 327) saw off an attempt to divide Christianity between Athanasians and Arians. But he fatally divided his empire between his three sons. The last known Roman Emperor to rule an undivided empire was Theodosius the Great who died in AD 395, and he only obtained this dubious distinction after a terrible defeat at Adrianople.

In the difficult fourth and fifth centuries the Balkans were threatened from the north and divided between East and West. Modern Dalmatia, where Diocletian ended his days, and modern Albania are very close to Italy. They fell under Venetian influence in the later Middle Ages. To this day they retain traces of Italian domination. By every right they had more claims than distant Britain to be involved in the Western half of the Empire, but boundaries have to be drawn somewhere, and sometimes the Adriatic formed the boundary between the East and the West. The threat from the north meant a large force of soldiers along the Danube frontier. Such soldiers continued to speak Latin, and Romanian speakers today attest the continuity of Latin, as do the Balkan Vlachs. Greek-speakers in the West lasted less strongly with Greek collapsing as a language of civilisation under the pressure of the barbarian invasions.

Diocletian's decision to divide the Roman Empire left an unhappy legacy along the dividing line. Many of the present troubles of Western Europe can be charged against his account. With Split as an epicentre we can see, as well as real earthquakes (which have affected Salonica and the Ionian Islands, Skopje and the Dalmatian coast within recent years) political upheavals along Diocletian's border.

The collapse of the Western Roman Empire in 476 did not make a complete break. There were still Latin-speakers in the Eastern Roman Empire, and one of them, Justinian, briefly reconquered some of the West. But then came the Slav invasions of the sixth and seventh centuries, most powerful along the Diocletian line, and then the religious division between Catholic and Orthodox which split the Slav invaders, with the Serbs and Bulgars opting for orthodoxy and the Cyrillic alphabet, while the Croats and Slovenes preferred the Latin rite and letters. Some stood confused, betwixt and between, speaking neither language like the Albanians or choosing another rite like the Bogomil heretics. There was clearly a no man's land between Greek and Latin, and it was there that Islam found most converts and we find most fragments.

After the Slav invasion there was a time when most of the northern Balkans was occupied by a loosely-knit Bulgarian Empire, but the Byzantines recovered and ruled almost all the Balkans in the eleventh and twelfth centuries. The Fourth Crusade shattered this empire, and in the next two and a half centuries we find, apart from the artificial and short-lived Latin Empire of Constantinople, brief periods of domination by the Second Bulgarian Empire of the Asenids and the Serbian Empire of the Nemanjids. The Ottomans conquered all the Balkans by the end of the fifteenth century, but gradually lost control of the northern half to the Hapsburgs in the seventeenth and eighteenth centuries. The nineteenth century saw the rise of nationalism with small national states beginning to be carved out of the declining Turkish realm, but until 1878 most of the Balkans were still under nominal Ottoman rule, and it was not until 1913 that they were expelled from the central swathe of Albania, Kosovo, Macedonia, northern Greece and southern Bulgaria, with which most of the chapters of this book are concerned.

Thus for most of history the Balkans have been under the domination of one empire or another. The advance of Austro-Hungary to include first Croatia and then Bosnia produced a shifting boundary between the Ottoman and Hapsburg Empires that was different from the Diocletian line but went through many of the same areas. The struggle between the Hapsburg and Ottoman Empires produced many strange fragments in the northern Balkans, the subject perhaps of another book; isolated Turks stranded on islands in the Danube and villages with French names on the Banat, relics of Maria Theresa's Alsatian frontier guards, are two colourful examples. Oddly the Banat, though an ethnic mosaic as fragmented as Macedonia, has never caused so much strife.[3]

Both the Hapsburgs and the Ottomans ruled over a multi-ethnic state, as did the Byzantine emperors and the rulers of the short-lived Bulgarian and Serbian Empires. Yugoslavia between 1918 and 1992 was a multi-ethnic state, as was Russia in both Czarist and Communist days. Even President Yeltsin's new Russia is multi-ethnic, although it makes no claims to the vast parts of Eastern Europe dominated by Russia since the time of Napoleon. These claims are left to others. During the Second World War Hitler's Third Reich ruled briefly, either directly or through puppet states, most of the Balkans, leaving odd fragments to Mussolini's rather pathetic attempt to create a new Roman Empire.

Empire is now a dirty word. Hitler and Mussolini have not helped it. In her long and still sadly relevant account of Yugoslavia, *Black Lamb and Grey Falcon*, Rebecca West shows why imperialism is wrong.[4] She was writing between 1936 and 1939 at a time when Abyssinia and Czechoslovakia had suffered the evil of imperial ambitions. She is rightly contemptuous of the Hapsburg ineptitude that had led to the Archduke's murder at Sarajevo and of the Ottoman incompetence that had led to the spiritual and moral inertia of southern Yugoslavia. She is oddly tolerant of the Serbs who between the wars had under Alexander Karageorgević virtually established a Serbian Empire over Yugoslavia, and there are not many criticisms by her of our own British Empire. The latter omission is not surprising; British schoolchildren in 1939 were still taught to celebrate Empire Day as the politically

correct equivalent of a lesson on the evils of Imperialism
in 1993.

Like the British Empire, the Roman Empire has few
defenders. And yet in both it was possible for the most
vulnerable civilians to travel in safety from one end of a
province to another. Even the Hapsburgs provided the
trappings of civilisation, as Croats have not forgotten,
though the Ottomans too before their fatal decline set such
a high standard of justice, compassion and strong government that lawless Balkan communities hastened to make
their submission. Yugoslavia was happier under Tito and
even the Karageorgević dynasty than it is now, Byzantium
in spite of Gibbon was a model of enlightenment and
tolerance; but before one begins praising Mussolini for
getting the trains to run on time, it is as well to dwell with
Rebecca West on the evils of empire.

Empires are evil when they impose, usually by force,
sometimes through persuasion, one way of life for another,
often in the process destroying or corrupting an aboriginal
culture, religion or language, presuming that the imperial
power is superior. The imperial invasion can take many
forms and leave many legacies. The straight lines of imperial boundary-makers in Africa, still preserved in modern
African states, are very different from the shifting con-
torted boundaries of the Hapsburg, Ottoman and Russian
Empires and the nation states that succeeded them. The
break up of the empires left odd fragments behind. The
larger the fragment, the more dangerous the legacy. Beleaguered Russians in the Baltic republics like the beleaguered Boers in South Africa are liable to cause more
trouble than white settlers in Kenya or some of the fragments whom I have described.

'Why mangle maggots when you could be murdering
men.' So might run an imaginary Balkan proverb, very
suitable to these times when people seem to have forgotten

the future in the murderous present, sanctified by a mythical past. This book has little to say about the future, but it does suggest that the present cannot be controlled by the past, and that national ideologies like imperial mythologies probably do more harm than good. Of course the pathetic though admirable myths propounded by, for example, the Vlachs of Slobozia or the extreme Muslim Pomaks provide some kind of comfort in a difficult age. Of course imperialism has bred resentment, and resentment has bred revenge. Major stakeholders in the revenge handicap have already declared their hand, in Ulster, in the Basque country, in Yugoslavia, in the Caucasus. This book is a plea to the minor fragmentary stakeholders to declare a different hand.

Notes

Chapter 1: Fragments

1. This phenomenon is well explained in P. Trudgill, 'Ausbau sociolinguistics and the perception of language status in contemporary Europe', *International Journal of Applied Linguistics*, 2 (2) (1992), pp. 167-78.

2. Perhaps most notably in the Jura. See E. Wiegandt, 'The Jura question: a challenge to Swiss ethnic peace', in D. Howell, ed., *Roots of Rural Ethnic Mobilisation* (Dartmouth, 1992), pp. 221-48.

3. R. Hindley, *The Death of the Irish Language* (London, 1990), pp. 229-34.

4. See Chapter 7.

5. A. Moritsch and G. Baumgartner, 'The process of national differentiation within rural communities in southern Carinthia and southern Burgenland, 1850-1940' in Howell, pp. 99-144.

6. See Chapter 4. E. Scarlatou, 'La romanité balkanique: origines et diffusion', *Revue des Etudes Sud-Est Européenes* xxix, 3-4 (1991), pp. 191-202, gives between 400,000 and 600,000, with half this number in Greece, 70,000-100,000 in Albania, 30,000-50,000 in Yugoslavia, 10,000-15,000 in Bulgaria and 80,000-100,000 in Romania.

7. F. Coulmas, ed., *Linguistic Minorities and Literacy* (New York, 1984).

8. The map is entitled *Approaching a Europe of the Languages* and is published by Ciemen (Barcelona, 1991). Maps showing boundaries are bound to distort the truth particularly in areas like the Balkans, where there is bilingualism, migration and large areas of uninhabited mountain. In Map 1 I cautiously avoid boundaries but have mistakenly omitted Gallego.

9. A shortened version of this chapter was orginally presented at the Nineteenth International Congress of the International Federation for Modern Languages and Literatures in Brasilia, September, 1993.

Chapter 2: Balkan Latinity

1. J. Wilkes, 'Arthur Evans in the Balkans, 1875-81', *Bulletin No 13 of the Institute of Archaeology* (1976), pp. 25-56.

2. Much of what follows can be found in T. Winnifrith, *The Vlachs* (London, 1987). Most scholarship on the Vlachs since that date has concentrated on the modern period. There have been rather fanciful attempts by A. Risos, 'The Vlachs of Larissa in the 10th Century', *Byzantoslavica*, 51 (1990), pp. 202-7 and, 'Die Vlachen und Pitta', *Byzantoslavica*, 53 (1992), pp. 233-6 to prove an Italian origin for the Vlachs. There is also a useful collection of articles in Centre d'Etude des Civilisations de l'Europe Centrale et du Sud-Est, Cahier No 8, *Les Aroumains*, in particular an admirable summary of the evidence from the Middle Ages by P. Nasturel, 'Les Valaques de l'éspace byzantin et bulgare jusqu'à la conquête ottomane', pp. 47-80.

3. Winnifrith, *The Vlachs*, pp. 49-50 for the Jireček line.

4. Gothic would appear to have had the postpositive article, as do the Scandinavian languages today. Risos's assumption that tenth century 'italiotai' in Thessaly are Italian ancestors of modern Vlachs appears to ignore the difference between Western and Eastern Romance with regard to the article.

5. Constantine Porphyrogenitus, *De Administrando Imperio*, ed. G. Moravczik and R. Jenkins (Budapest, 1949).

6. H. Holland, *Travels in the Ionian Isles, Albania, Thessaly, Macedonia, etc* (London, 1815) has many mentions of Strabo, but his map seems to have one lake north of Ohrid, one lake in the Kastoria district and no lake Prespa at all.

7. J. Lampe and M. Jackson, *Balkan Economic History, 1550-1950* (Indiana, 1982), pp. 43-5 for Vlach and Greek migration northwards and the fact that the language of commerce was Greek.

8. *Mémoire Presenté par les Délégues Valaques d'Epire et de Thessalie aux Ambassadeurs à Constantinople* (Pera, 1881).

9. It was at a congress at Bitola under the chairmanship of Midhat Frasheri in 1908 that the problem of the Albanian alphabet was virtually solved with Latin characters winning over the Ottoman, Greek and Cyrillic scripts. Vlach congresses occasionally debate the alphabet; there are of course Vlachs who only know the Greek alphabet, and a few who only know the Cyrillic letters, but the main debate now is between those who would adopt the Romanian alphabet in its entirety, and those who would adopt a few new diacritical signs.

10. A. Wace and M. Thompson, *The Nomads of the Balkans* (London, 1914) reprinted 1972, translated into Greek with additional notes by N. Kazanes (Salonica, 1987).

11. A. Lazarou, *L'Aroumain et ses rapports avec le Grec* (Salonica, 1986) originally written in Greek (Athens, 1976), gives the best statement of this view.

12. The paper from this conference was published in D. Howell, ed., *Roots of Rural Ethnic Mobilization* (Dartmouth, 1992), pp. 277-304.

13. This chapter was originally given as a paper at a conference on Romanian National Identity at the University of London in September, 1992, and with further additions at a conference on Greek Minorities at St Anne's College, Oxford, January, 1994. Map 2 shows the Vlachs in the context of medieval history.

Chapter 3: The Vlach Diaspora

1. For an account of this village see T. Winnifrith, *The Vlachs* (London, 1987), p. 16 and G. Moran, 'Touring the Vlach Villages of Greece', *Newsletter of the Society Farsarotul* VI,I, an invaluable account from an American Vlach of the present position in Greece.

2. *The Vlachs*, p. 31. Disappointingly in 1992 the snow melted.

3. See Map 3. Details of this map are taken from the statistical tables in J. Trifunoski, *Bitolsko – Prilepskata Kotlena* (Skopje, 1970) and may be out of date. It is, however, an invaluable guide to the mixed composition of a small area of southern Yugoslav Macedonia. Included in the map for the sake of completeness are a few Vlach villages in Greece; off the map to the south-west are Doliana, Delvinaki, Visani and Parakalamos, Vlach villages that Moran found but I did not mention in *The Vlachs*.

4. As shown above the newsletter of this Society is an invaluable source of information about the Vlachs, and the Society has played a valuable part in establishing links with Vlachs in nations like Romania and Albania.

5. *Frandza Vlaha* is less scholarly than *the Newsletter of the Society Farsarotul* but can, as can *Zborlu Nostru*, throw up the occasional item of interest.

6. This was of course just before the opening up of Albania to the beginnings of democracy in 1991 and real democracy in 1992.

7. These, emerging in 1990, as seen in the Newsletter of that year, appear to have been fortunately resolved.

8. According to Moran the village has both names and is deserted.

9. *Newsletter of the Society Farsarotul* IV, 2 (1990).

10. In late 1993 the dinar has just slumped from two billion to the mark to five billion, and is probably slumping further as I write with the number of noughts increasingly eliminated and irrelevant.

Chapter 4: Vlachs in Albania

1. G. Weigand in *Die Aromunen* (Leipzig, 1884), p. 111 mentions Boboshticë as Bulgarian and marks it and the neighbouring Drenovë as Bulgarian on his map, although he did not actually visit either village. A. Mazon, *Documents, Contes et Chansons Slaves de l'Albanie du Sud* (Paris, 1936) gives quite an ancient Bulgarian history for the

two villages, mentioning Greek, Turkish and Albanian but not Vlach as rival languages.

2. If Weigand and Mazon are right, the Vlach-speakers of Boboshticë are recent arrivals. The Second World War, in which neighbouring Macedonia was occupied by Bulgaria and there were ferocious Partisan campaigns, presumably involved many forcible exchanges of population, and the Hoxha regime introduced much resettlement, some of it, as in the case of the Vlachs of Andon Poçi, quite benevolent.

3. I. Martianos, *Hē Moschopolis, 1330-1930* (Salonica, 1957) and S. Adhami, *Voskopoja* (Tirana, 1989) give the Greek and Albanian points of view.

4. N. Hammond, *Epirus* (Oxford, 1967), p. 231 and H. Holland, *Travels in the Ionian Isles, Albania, Thessaly, Macedonia, etc* (London, 1815), p. 519. We were shown the mines, now sadly not working.

5. T. Winnifrith, *The Vlachs* (London, 1987), p. 35.

6. Weigand says that the Vlach villages in this area are small. A. Tamas, 'La Romaine et la minorité roumaine en Albanie', *Voix des Peuples Minorités 5* (1938), pp. 79-89 says that they are losing their Vlach identity. Few of the maps in H. Wilkinson, *Maps and Politics* (Liverpool, 1951) pay much attention to Vlachs on the coast, and those that do clearly exaggerate their influence. My own researches in 1993 are recorded later in this chapter and Map 4.

7. Figures for minorities in Albania are particularly unreliable. See note 11 for exaggerated Greek claims. J. Pettifer, *The Blue Guide to Albania* (London, 1994), pp. 72-4 estimates 40,000 to 200,000 Greeks, 50,000 Vlachs, up to 100,000 Gypsies, 10,000-15,000 Slavs and a few hundred Armenians. Bilingualism is quite common and quite hard to detect: years of caution have taught Albanians to conceal their skills. S. Horak, *East European National Minorities* (Colorado, 1985) gives very cautiously 35,000 Greeks, 35,000 Vlachs, 10,000 Slavs and 5000 Gypsies.

8. I conducted a rudimentary linguistic test on an inhabitant of Selenicë and an inhabitant of Voskopojë. Both seemed to speak much the same kind of Vlach. In particular the word for horse, *cau*, amusingly and confusingly pronounced cow, would seem an Albanian Vlach idiosyncrasy.

9. Moran also reports only one village in this area, but in addition to Morphi near Parga the Kramer-Dahmen team also report Vlach villages near Igoumenitsa, like Perdika, Plataria, Katavothra and Karvounari, and this was confirmed by Albanians.

10. I have been unable to find in the Korcë area Shengerj, in the Durrës area Shenavlash, in the Lushnjë area Frakull, in the Berat area Vovjodë, in the Vlorë area Besnist, Zavalinë, in the Permet area Trebozisht, Ogdunan, Lilarisht, in the Ersekë area Lengas and Tridhjetdyshe.

11. *Independent*, Tuesday August 17th, 1993.

12. The maps of V. Diamandi (pre-Balkan wars), A. Atanasiu (1919), M. Marioteanu in *Dialectologie Romana* (Bucharest, 1977) and B. Trpkoski-Trpki, *Blasete na Balkanot* (Skopje, 1986) are useful for tracking down villages, although there are always difficulties with names transliterated from one script to another, and often completely different in Vlach. In addition the last two maps would appear to rely heavily on earlier sources.

13. This chapter was originally given as a paper to the Society for South Eastern European Studies at the University of Bradford in November, 1993. In 1994 I made a brief visit to Vlach villages with impressive churches near Gjirokastër.

Chapter 5: Vlachs in Romania

1. Wace and Thompson suggest this impartially, and Greek sources confirm it.

2. M. Peyfuss, 'Aromunen in Rumanien', *Österreichische Osthefte* 26 (1984), pp. 313-19 and 'Les Aroumains a l'ère des nationalismes balkaniques', *Centre d'Etude des Civilizations de l'Europe Centrale et du Sud-Est* 8 (1989), pp. 129-49 is very informative.

3. See Chapter 1 for a brief resumé of these two difficult areas, oddly free from inter-ethnic strife, perhaps because of frequent changes of frontier, perhaps because of constant migration, perhaps because of the multiplicity of races. Both would repay a detailed investigation.

4. The Germans have now left. The Serbians, being Orthodox, intermarried with both Vlachs and Romanians.

5. The present state of Moldova does not coincide with the province of Bessarabia, but is still a linguistic medley. See M. Cazacu and N. Trifon, *La Moldavie ex-Soviétique: histoire et enjeux actuels* (Paris, 1993).

6. Notably N. Saramandu, *Cercetare asupra Aromanei Vorbite in Dobrogea* (Bucharest, 1972) on whose map I have drawn for Map 5. I am also grateful to M. Caragiu Marioteanu, N.S. Tanasoca and E. Scarlatou for help and hospitality. Peyfuss in 'Aromunen in Rumanien' gives the official figures for the 1977 census as 644 Aromanians and 1179 Macedoromanians, but these are clearly far too low, since most Vlachs would call themselves Romanians. He also says that in addition to the Gramosteani and Farsheroti there are groups calling themselves Pindeni (from the Pindus), Moscopoleni and Muzacheari (from Albania). Scarlatou has done valuable linguistic work among Meglen Vlachs in the Dobrudja. A 1992 census gave 21,089 Aromanians and 6,999 Macedoromanians.

7. On the Greek border between Florina and Bitola can be found rather pathetically Neos Kaukasos and the more triumphant Niki. The

Vlach villages in the Dobrudja do not seem to have transferred names with their migration.

8. P. Trudgill, 'The Ausbau sociolinguistics of Greece', *Plurilinguismus* 4 (June, 1992), pp. 167-91.

9. P. Trudgill and G. Tzavaros, 'A sociolinguistic study of Albanian spoken in the Attica and Boiotia areas of Greece', *Report to the Social Science Research Council* (London, 1975).

10. See Chapters 4 and 7.

Chapter 6: The Pomaks

1. Torbesh in Yugoslavia, Goran in Albania. See Map 3 for the Torbesh villages, although this is based on a 1951 investigation.

2. Just to complicate the picture there are Turkish-speaking Christians (the Gagauz) and Christian Gypsies, whose languages are too baffling to be summarised, although a British diplomat, B. Gilliat Smith, serving in Varna in the First World War, did almost master the problem of the Gypsy dialects of Bulgaria.

3. Perhaps not quite so happily as, since I wrote this, the Bulgarian government has broken down.

4. J. Seypell, 'Pomaks in northeastern Greece: an endangered Balkan population', *International Institute of Muslim Minority Affairs* 10,1 (January, 1989), pp. 41-9, gives an excellent if slightly anecdotal account of the Pomaks in Greece.

5. Exact numbers are impossible to calculate in either Albania or Yugoslavia at the moment owing to the flood of refugees out of Albania for economic reasons and into Yugoslav Macedonia for political reasons. Figures of 20,000 for the Slav-speaking population of Albania (G. Klein and M. Reban, eds, *The Politics of Ethnicity in Eastern Europe* (Columbia, 1981) p. 41), and Muslims in Yugoslav Macedonia (40,000, 1981 census) are neither up-to-date, nor include all Pomaks, nor exclude some Slav-speaking non-Pomaks in Albania, and non-Slav-speaking Muslims in Yugoslavia. Figures for Pomaks in Greece and Bulgaria have been given after talking to impartial field workers. Again official census figures are hardly a guide, for obvious reasons. The *Longman Directory of Minorities*, edited by the Minority Rights Group in London, gives the figure of 150,000 Pomaks in Bulgaria, but no evidence for this figure.

6. Professor Konstantinov said that the camel's head, the lost stone and the confusion between the birth of Christ and the flight of Mahomet are common features of many Muslim villages anxious to establish their antiquity.

7. Seypell gives the relevant bibliography. As with so many Balkan controversies it is unfortunate that there is little impartial study of the

Pomaks, and rather less study of the Pomaks by themselves. Map 6 is a very rough-and-ready affair for both Greece and Bulgaria.

8. E. Gibbon, *Decline and Fall of the Roman Empire* (Oxford, 1966) Vol. VI, pp. 464-5 for the defeat, death and legendary survival of Baldwin. All over the Balkans the melancholy present is temporarily relieved by fantasies from the past to the effect that Prince Lazar or Marko Kraljević or Alexander the Great or Saint Demetrius or Achilles is not dead but sleepeth, and will awaken to lead his people to a glorious victory.

9. They can be found in A. Karathanases, *Ho Hellēnismos kai hē Metropolē tou Nevrokopou kata ton Makedoniko Agōna* (Salonica, 1992). The fulminations of the bishop are similar to those of Demosthenes against Philip and Alexander, although delivered from a rather different quarter.

10. For Yuruks see Wilkinson, *Maps and Politics* (Liverpool, 1951). Wilkinson is an invaluable guide to the vagaries of Balkan ethnic patterns as depicted by map makers, either ignorant of the true facts, or with an axe to grind, or with both of these disadvantages. Unfortunately his work is now forty years old and his main area of concentration is a little too far west for the Pomaks.

Chapter 7: Greek Fragments

1. H. Wilkinson, *Maps and Politics* (Liverpool, 1951) includes some information about Greek minorities. S. Nestor, 'Greek Macedonia and the Convention of Neuilly', *Balkan Studies 3* (1962), pp. 169-84 and S. Ladas, *The Exchange of Minorities: Bulgaria, Greece and Turkey* (New York, 1932) provide details of population exchanges.

2. In Venizelos, the architect of the population exchanges, Greece had a great statesman who was prepared to accept a defeat for which he had not been responsible and to turn its consequences (a vast immigrant population from lost territories) into something like victory. It is difficult to see anyone of the same stature in the Balkans today. If Serbia had been defeated she might theoretically have been persuaded to accept Serb refugees from Croatia and Bosnia (hardly Kosovo) in exchange for Croats and Bosnian Muslims living in Serbia, but there are very few Croats or Bosnians in Serbia which was not defeated.

3. Wilkinson, pp. 261-73.

4. See Chapter 4. Pamphlets stating either side of the case (with the Albanians being very conciliatory) may be obtained from the Secretary of the Friends of Albania.

5. H. Holland, *Travellers in the Ionian Isles, Albania, Thessaly, Macedonia etc* (London 1815), pp. 434, 480.

6. P. Ruchas, *Albania's Captives* (Chicago, 1965).

7. A good article with satisfactory bibliography on the decline of

Greek in southern Italy is that by M. Katsoyannou, 'Mort des langues et locuteurs terminales: le cas de la minorité grécophone de la Calabre (Italie)', *Plurilinguismus* 4 (June, 1992), pp. 84-111. I visited Apulia in 1982 and found a few old people speaking an extraordinary kind of Greek, much despised by progressives busily learning standard Greek.

8. P. Mackridge, 'A transhumance', *Oxford Magazine*, 8th week Hilary Term, 1988, pp. 6-7. R. Dawkins before the war in *Modern Greek in Asia Minor* (Cambridge, 1917) gives fascinating accounts of the ways in which Greeks in remote parts of Anatolia preserved their language in a form virtually amalgamated with Turkish. Some had already converted to Islam and were losing their language in the process, thus rendering the survival of Greek in these remote parts unlikely.

9. *The Longman Directory of Minorities* (London, 1992) probably erring on the side of generosity gives the figure of displaced Greeks in the Soviet Union as 400,000. See R. Browning, *Medieval and Modern Greek* (London, 1969), p. 132, for the strange dialects of Mariupol.

10. Bulgarian census figures of 1965 are recorded in S. Horak, *East European National Minorities* (Colorado, 1985), p. 281.

11. The number of Sarakatsans in the 1965 census cannot really be calculated from the 8,241 Greeks and 763 Romanians. 15,000 is an estimate I have heard.

12. A good account of the Boliaric language in Greece can be found in P. Leigh Fermor, *Roumeli: Travels in Northern Greece* (London, 1966), esp pp. 237-40. For the Balkans as a whole see B. Sikimić, 'Balkan secret languages versus modern slang', *Revue des Etudes Sud-Est Européenes* xxx 3-4 (1992), pp. 275-80.

13. A Choralampoulos, *Phonologikē Analysē tēs Tsakonikēs Dialektou* (Salonica, 1980).

14. Armenians have always been present in Europe since Byzantine times. M. Nystazopoulou-Pelekidou, *The Macedonian Question* (Corfu, 1992), p. 15 quotes a census of 1941 with 80,000 Armenians. She disagrees with this census. See note 23.

15. The 1941 census shows 74,000 Laz. In turn the *Longman Directory* maintains that there are a large number of Greeks as well as Laz in Georgia. In actual fact lack of contact between Greece and the Caucasus would mean that most members of these minorities would have lost their language and their special identity fairly rapidly.

16. P. Trudgill, 'The Ausbau sociolinguistics of Greece', *Plurilinguismus* 4 (June, 1992), pp. 167-91.

17. Kolettis, the first prime minister of Greece, and various members of the Averoff family are the most obvious examples.

18. Trudgill makes no distinction between the Albanians near the border and the Albanians in Attica and Boiotia, the latter linguistically and culturally long separated from Albania, though subject to no persecution. The two kinds of Albanian are worthy of study, although the problem is now complicated by the flood of refugees into Greece from Albania.

19. The Institute for Balkan Studies regularly produces histories of these former enclaves of Hellenism, e.g. that by A. Agellopoulos on Strumica (1985), A. Karathanases on Nevrokop (1991), L. Kamperidis on Sozopolis on the Black Sea Coast (1993).

20. See Chapter 6.

21. A. Iordanoglou, *To Ethnikon Ioakeimeion Parthenagōgeion Konstantinoupoleōs* (Salonica, 1989) shows the decline.

22. *The Drama of the Moslem Minority in Western Thrace*, an anonymous work published in 1983 by the Association of Solidarity with Western Thrace, Turks in Germany and Turkey gives a one-sided picture. There is a full bibliography in X. Kotzageorgē and A. Panagiotopoulou, *Neoterē kai Sunchronē Historia tēs Thrakēs: Bibliographikos Hodēgos* (Salonica, 1993).

23. At a conference in Oxford in January 1994 organised by Richard Clogg there was further discussion of minorities, including such religious minorities as Catholics and Protestants. I have not been able to incorporate many of the findings of this conference which will, it is hoped, be published shortly.

Chapter 8: Macedonia

1. The reference may be found in N.P. Andriotes, *The Language and the Greek Origin of the Ancient Macedonians* (Salonica, 1979), p. 31.

2. Greek propaganda in insisting that Alexander and Philip spoke Greek tends to ignore the evidence of Demosthenes that both were barbarians, but Demosthenes himself was a propagandist rather than a philologist, and it is possible to dismiss his jibes as sneers against provincialism.

3. There are few histories of Greece under Roman rule, itself a fact that proves stagnation.

4. His *De Aedificiis* shows Justinian's defences against the Slavs, but in spite of the work of V. Besevliev, *Zur Deutung der Kastellnamen in Prokop's Werk 'De Aedificiis'* (Amsterdam, 1970) it is still not possible to see how far these defences were successful, or indeed where and when they were set up.

5. See Map 8.

6. E. Kofos, 'The making of Yugoslavia's People's Republic of Macedonia', *Balkan Studies* 3 (1962), pp. 375-96 gives a fair account of the setting up of this province; although he writes from the Greek point of view, he was writing when there was less political tension.

7. See Chapter 1, note 1.

8. T. Winnifrith, *The Vlachs*, p. 120.

9. A Vlach association in Kruševo calls itself after Pitor Guli, who fought with Goce Delčev in 1902.

10. H. Wilkinson, *Maps and Politics*, pp. 172-82 for Cvijić's changing views.

11. These figures are taken from the 1981 census. Greek sources make great play with the number of Albanians in Macedonia, their figure of 35 per cent being almost certainly too high and achieved by lumping together all non-Macedonians. On the other hand there are factors increasing the number of Albanians and probably some pressure in 1981 to declare oneself Macedonian. See Map 8. A census was held in July 1994 for Macedonia.

12. These figures from the 1981 census are obviously and tragically out of date.

13. As in most large towns there are a large number of immigrants. There are Albanian villages near Skopje and a famous Gypsy quarter in the town.

14. R. Shannon, *Gladstone and the Bulgarian Agitaion, 1876* (London, 1963).

15. I write this chapter just as the countries of the European Community in December 1993 have finally recognised FYROM. Events in the next months are likely to render prophecy futile, although they cannot alter history.

Chapter 9: Kosovo

1. C. Imber, *The Ottoman Empire* 1300-1481 (Istanbul, 1990), pp. 35-6 citing T. Emmert, *The Battle of Kosovo: A Reconsideration of its Significance in the Decline of Medieval Serbia* (Ann Arbor, 1973). Both these works were written before the break up of Yugoslavia, whereas anti-Serbian feeling may have begun to influence some of the essays in W.S. Vucinich and T. Emmert, eds, *Kosovo: Legacy of a Medieval Battle* (Minneapolis, 1991).

2. This poetic image is helped by the fact that Kosovar Albanians wear white skull caps, while Montenegro means black mountain, and the Karageorgević dynasty is the family of Black George.

3. Kosovo was an autonomous province in Serbia from 1946 until 1989. Greater autonomy was granted in 1968.

4. Unlike the *Iliad* and the *Odyssey* the Serbian lays are not easily available in translation, but N. Curcija-Proadanovic, *Heroes of Serbia* (Oxford, 1965) translates some, and there is a literal translation in M. Parry and A. Lord, *Sprsko-Hrvatrske Junacke Pesme* (Harvard and Belgrade, 1953).

5. E. Durham mentions the Vlachs of Priština and Macedonia in *High Albania* (London, 1909) pp. 286, 297. For the ambiguous references to Vlachs in the fourteenth-century Statutes of Dečani see T. Winnifrith, *Perspectives on Albania* (London, 1992), p. 8.

6. E. Babcock and C. Krey, *A History of Deeds Done beyond the Sea* (Columbia, 1943, Vol. ii, pp. 348-9, although the reference here to a campaign against the Serbs, from which the Emperor Manuel retired to Bitola, may not show much Serb penetration into Macedonia.

7. D. Nicol, *The Despotate of Epiros, 1267-1479* (Cambridge, 1984) gives plenty of examples of Serbian involvement in northern Greece, although the exact ethnicity of people who are described as Serbalbanitovlachs is obscure.

8. See T. Winnifrith, *Perspectives on Albania* (London, 1992) pp. 12-13.

9. B. Spiridonakis, *Grecs, Occidentaux et Turcs de 1054 à 1453* (Salonica, 1990) shows how in the fourteenth and fifteenth centuries Ottoman armies were regularly helped by Serbs, Albanians and even Greeks.

10. A. Lopasic, 'Cultural values of the Albanians in the Diaspora' in T. Winnifrith, *Perspectives on Albania*, pp. 89-105.

11. In 1981 Kosovo had 1,584,440 inhabitants, Slovenia 1,891,864, Macedonia 1,909,112, Montenegro 584,310. In 1948 the population of Kosovo was only 733,034.

Chapter 10: Shattered Eagles

1. The Hapsburg double eagle presumably goes back to the time when the Hapsburgs were Holy Roman Emperors. I do not know why Scanderbeg adopted it as his crest, although it was clearly a good symbol for the Albanian land which calls itself Shqiperia, land of the eagle.

2. In the *Sunday Times* of August 9, 1992 Professor N. Stone first drew attention to Diocletian's fatal flaw as symbolised by the double eagle.

3. Prosperity, mixed marriages and the sheer multiciplicity of races may explain this peaceful state of affairs.

4. R. West, *Black Lamb and Grey Falcon* (London, 1942).

Select Bibliography

Adhami, S., *Voskopoja* (Tirana, 1989).

Andriotes, N., *The Language and Greek Origin of the Ancient Macedonians* (Salonica, 1979).

Angelolopoulos, A., 'Population distribution of Greece today according to language, national consciousness and religion', *Balkan Studies* 20 (1979), 123-32.

Anon., *Memoire presenté par les délégues Valaques d'Epire et de Thessalie aux ambassadeurs à Constantinople* (Pera, 1881).

Besevliev, V., *Zur Deutung der Kastellnamen in Prokops Werk 'De Aedificiis'* (Amsterdam, 1970)

Browning, R., *Medieval and Modern Greek* (London, 1969).

Campbell, J., *Honour, Family and Patronage* (Oxford, 1964).

Capidan, T., *Les Macédo-Roumains* (Bucharest, 1937).

Cazacu, M. & Trifon, N., *La Moldavie ex-soviétique: histoire et enjeux actuels* (Paris, 1993).

Chorolampoulos, A., *Phonologikē Analysē tēs Tsakonikēs Dialektou* (Salonica, 1980).

Chrysochoos, M., *Blachoi kai Koutsovlachoi* (Athens, 1909).

Coulmas, F., ed., *Linguistic Minorities and Literacy* (New York, 1984).

Constantine Porphyrogenitus, *De Administrando Imperio*, ed. G. Moravczik & R. Jenkins (Budapest, 1949).

Cvijić, J., *La Peninsule Balkanique* (Paris, 1918).

Dahmen, W. & Kramer, J., eds, *Balkan Archiv* (Hamburg, 1976-94).

Dakin, D., *The Greek Struggle in Macedonia, 1897-1913* (Salonica, 1966).

——, *The Unification of Greece, 1770-1923* (London, 1972).

Daskalakis, A., *The Hellenism of the Ancient Macedonians* (Salonica, 1965).

Dawkins, R., *Modern Greek in Asia Minor* (Cambridge, 1917).

Durham, E., *High Albania* (London, 1908).

——, *Twenty Years of Balkan Tangle* (London, 1920).

Evans, A., *Through Bosnia and Herzogovina* (London, 1877).

Fernandes-Armesto, F., *The Tribes of Europe* (London, 1994).

Fine, J., *The Early Medieval Balkans* (Michigan, 1983).

——, *The Late Medieval Balkans* (Michigan, 1987).

162   Bibliography

Fortis, A., *Travels into Dalmatia* (London, 1778).
Gibbon, E., *Decline and Fall of the Roman Empire* (Oxford, 1966).
Glenny, M., *The Fall of Yugoslavia: The Third Balkan War* (London, 1992).
Hammond, N., *Epirus* (Oxford, 1967).
——, *A History of Macedonia*, vol. 1 (Oxford, 1972).
——, *Migrations and Invasions in Greece and Adjacent Areas* (New Jersey, 1976).
—— & Griffith, G., *A History of Macedonia*, vol. 2 (Oxford, 1979).
—— & Walbank, F., *A History of Macedonia*, vol. 3 (Oxford, 1988).
Hindley, R., *The Death of the Irish Language* (London, 1990).
Hoeg, C., *Les Saracatsans* (Paris & Copenhagen, 1925-6).
Holland, H., *Travels in the Ionian Isles, Albania, Thessaly, Macedonia etc.* (London, 1815).
Horak, S., *East European National Minorities* (Colorado, 1985).
Howell, D., *Roots of Rural Ethnic Mobilisation* (Dartmouth, 1992).
Iordanoglou, A., *To Ethnikon Ioakeimeion Parthenagōgeion Konstanti-noupoleōs* (Salonica, 1989).
Jelavich, B., *History of the Balkans* (Cambridge, 1983).
Karathanases, A., *Ho Hellēnismos kai hē Metropolē tou Nevrokopou kata ton Makedoniko Agōna* (Salonica, 1992).
Katsoyannou, M., 'Mort des langues et locuteurs terminales: le cas de la minorité grécophone de la Calabre (Italie)', *Plurilinguismus* 4 (June, 1992), 84-111.
Katsoyiannes, T., *Peri tōn Blachōn ton Hellēnikōn Chōrōn* (Salonica, 1974).
Keramopoulos, A., *Ti Einai hoi Koutsoblachoi* (Athens, 1938).
Klein, G. & Reban, M., eds, *The Politics of Ethnicity in Eastern Europe* (Columbia, 1981)
Kofos, E., 'The making of Yugoslavia's People's Republic of Macedonia', *Balkan Studies* 3 (1962), 375-6.
Kotzageorgē, X. and Panagiotopoulou, A., *Neotorē kai Sunchronē Historia tēs Thrakēs: Bibliographikēs Hodēgos* (Salonica, 1993).
Ladas, S., *The Exchange of Minorities: Bulgaria, Greece and Turkey* (New York, 1932).
Lampe, J. & Jackson, M., *Balkan Economic History, 1550-1950* (Indiana, 1982).
Lazarou, A., *L'Aroumain et ses rapports avec le Grec* (Salonica, 1986).
Leigh Fermor, P., *Roumeli: Travels in Northern Greece* (London, 1966).
Mackridge, P., 'A transhumance', *Oxford Magazine*, 8th week, Hilary Term 1988, 6-7
Malcolm, N., *Bosnia: A Short History* (London, 1994).
Marmellaku, R., *Albania and the Albanians* (London, 1975).
Maroteanu, A., *Dialectologie Romana* (Bucharest, 1977).
Martianos, I., *Hē Moschopolis, 1330-1930* (Salonica, 1957).

Mazon, A., *Documents, Contes et Chansons, Slaves de l'Albanie du sud* (Paris, 1936).

Moritsch, A. & Baumgarter, G., 'The process of national differentiation within rural communities in Southern Carinthia and Southern Burgenland' in D. Howell, ed., *Roots of Rural Ethnic Mobilization* (Dartmouth, 1992), 99-144.

Nasturel, P., 'Les Valaques de l'espace byzantin et bulgare jusqu'à la conquête ottomane', *Centre d'Étude des Civilisations de l'Europe Centrale et du Sud-Est*, Cahier no. 8, 47-80.

Nestor, S., 'Greek Macedonia and the Convention of Neuilly', *Balkan Studies* 3 (1962), 169-84.

Nicol, D., *The Despotate of Epirus, 1267-1479* (Cambridge, 1984).

Nystapoulou-Pelekidou, M., *The Macedonian Question* (Corfu, 1992).

Obolensky, D., *The Bogomils* (Cambridge, 1948).

——, *The Byzantine Commonwealth* (London, 1971).

Pentzopoulos, D., *The Balkan Exchange of Minorities and its Impact upon Greece* (Paris, 1962).

Pettifer, J., *The Blue Guide to Albania* (London, 1994).

Peyfuss, M., 'Aromunen in Rumanien', *Österreichische Osthefte*, 26 (1984), 313-19.

——, *Die Aromunische Frage* (Vienna, 1974).

——, 'Les Aroumains à l'ère des nationalismes balkaniques', *Centre d'Etude des Civilisations de l'Europe Centrale et du Sud-Est*, 8 (1989), 129-49.

Poulton, H., *The Balkans: States and Minorities in Conflict* (London, 1991).

Radojicić, D., ' "Bulgaraibanitoblahos" et "Serbalbanitobulgaroblahos" – deux caracteristiques ethniques de sud-est européen du xive et xve siècles', *Romanoslavica* 13 (1966), 72-9.

Risos, A., 'The Vlachs of Larissa in the 10th century', *Byzantoslavica*, 51 (1990), 207-17.

——, 'Die Vlachen und Pitta', *Byzantoslavica* 53 (1992), 233-6.

Ruchas, P., *Albania's Captives* (Chicago, 1965).

Runciman, S., *A History of the First Bulgarian Empire* (Oxford, 1932).

Saramandu, N., *Cercetari asupra Aromanei Vorbite in Dobrogea* (Bucharest, 1972).

Scarlatou, E., 'La Romanité Balkanique: origines et diffusion', *Revue des Etudes Sud-Est Européenes* xxix, 3-4 (1991), 191-202.

Seypell, J., 'Pomaks in Northeastern Greece: an endangered Balkan population', *International Institute of Muslim Minority Affairs* 10,1 (January 1989), 41-9.

Shaw, S., *History of the Ottoman Empire and Modern Turkey* (Cambridge, 1976).

Sikimić, B., 'Balkan street languages versus modern slang', *Revue des Etudes Sud-Est Européenes* xxx, 3-4 (1992), 275-80.

Spiridonakis, B., *Grecs, Occidentaux et Turcs de 1054 à 1453* (Salonica, 1990).

Sugar, P., *South Eastern Europe under Ottoman Rule, 1354-1804* (Seattle, 1977).

Tamas, A., 'La Romaine et la minorité roumaine en Albanie', *Voix des Peuples Minorités* 5 (1938), 79-89.

Trifunoski, J., *Bitolsko-Prilepskata Kotlena* (Skopje, 1970).

Trpkoski-Trpki, B., *Blasete na Balkanot* (Skopje, 1986).

Trudgill, P., 'Ausbau sociolinguistics and the perception of language status in contemporary Europe', *International Journal of Applied Linguistics* 2(2) (1992), 167-78.

——, 'The Ausbau sociolinguistics of Greece', *Plurilinguismus* 4 (June 1992), 167-91.

—— & Tzavaros, G., 'A sociolinguistic study of Albanian spoken in the Attica and Boiotia areas of Greece', *Report to the Social Science Research Council* (London, 1975).

Vakalopoulos, A., *Origins of the Greek Nation*, tr. I. Moles (Rutgers, 1970).

——, *The Greek Nation, 1453-1669*, tr. I. & P. Moles (Rutgers, 1976).

Vucinich, W & Emmert, T., eds, *Kosovo: Legacy of a Medieval Battle* (Minneapolis, 1991).

Wace, A. & Thompson, M., *The Nomads of the Balkans* (London, 1914).

Weigand, G., *Die Aromunen* (Leipzig, 1884).

West, R., *Black Lamb and Grey Falcon* (London, 1942).

Wiegandt, E., 'The Jura question: a challenge to Swiss ethnic peace' in D. Howell, ed., *Roots of Rural Ethnic Mobilisation* (Dartmouth, 1992), 221-48.

Wilkes, J., 'Arthur Evans in the Balkans, 1875-81', *Bulletin No. 13 of the Institute of Archaeology* (1976), 25-56.

——, *The Illyrians* (London, 1992).

Wilkinson, H., *Maps and Politics* (Liverpool, 1951).

Winnifrith, T., *The Vlachs: History of a Balkan People* (London, 1987).

——, ed., *Perspectives on Albania* (London, 1992)

Index